OFF THE ROPES

OFF THE ROPES
my story

ROLAND VANDAL
AS TOLD TO CARLENE RUMMERY

J. GORDON SHILLINGFORD
PUBLISHING INC

Off the Ropes: My Story
First published 2015 by J. Gordon Shillingford Publishing Inc.
© 2015, Roland Vandal

Cover and interior design by Relish New Brand Experience
Printed and bound in Canada on 100% post-consumer recycled paper

We acknowledge the financial support of the Manitoba Arts Council and The Canada Council for the Arts for our publishing program.

J. Gordon Shillingford Publishing
Box 86, RPO Corydon Avenue
Winnipeg, MB R3M 3S3

LIBRARY AND ARCHIVES CANADA CATALOGUING IN PUBLICATION

Vandal, Roland, 1971, author
    Off the ropes : my story / Roland Vandal.

ISBN 978-1-927922-09-5 (pbk.)

    1. Vandal, Roland, 1971-. 2. Boxers (Sports)--Canada--Biography. 3. Recovering addicts--Canada--Biography.
4. Post-traumatic stress disorder--Patients--Canada--Biography.
I. Title.

GV1132.V35A3 2015   796.83092   C2015-902121-9

Acknowledgements

The fact I even have a book in print baffles me. The process of writing the book was cathartic, and through the process, I've literally been able to turn the page on the darkest times of my life. To my friends and family, this journey would not have been possible without your support.

I want to thank my friend Geoff Kirbyson for putting me in contact with my publisher, Gordon Shilllingford. I am humbled by Gordon's interest, and appreciate how much he's invested in me. I am thankful for this opportunity.

Anyone appointed with the task of taking my free-thought writings and crafting it into a book is clearly worthy of a hearty thank you. Carlene Rummery, you have been patient with me, and I am very appreciative.

Darcie, thank you for typing out my chicken scratches, and for being a forever friend.

To my sons, Jesse and Jaicey, I love you both dearly. To all the teens in my youth home, each of you has taught me more about myself than I could have ever learned on my own. Jesse, thank you for spending hours sorting and compiling the photos for this book.

Thank you to Richard, Mitch, Harry, George, and my Uncle Dan. You are the most patient men I know. You are my father figures, and I love and respect everything you do. Every man should be so lucky as to have men like you to look up to and to emulate.

Thank you to my friends "Ken," Paul, Kent, Jennifer, Garnett, Ian, Colin, Cris, Monty, Jason, Mike, Carson, Victor, Amber,

Patty, Pamela, Rebecca, Onalee, Gillian, Alecia, Melanie, Michelle, Deanna, Al, Kristin, Kaley, and Beverly. Thank you Drew, Josh, and Jerimiah, and thank you to the community at Red Road Lodge Recovery Mission. Thank you Tracey, Leslie, Javen, Jason, and again, Jesse, for your support in my work with youth.

Thank you to my mother for doing the best she could with what she had. Respect and love to my father for being the conscience in my head, when you were with us, and since you've been gone. Thank you to all the families who took me in as one of their own. To the McJannetts, Malbrancks, Borsas, Winklers, Garretts, Labiuks, Whalens, and the Wrights, please know you all had an impact on my life. Thank you Aunt Jeanette, Scott and Crystal—you and Uncle Denis often gave me shelter from the storms I created.

Thanks too to Jim Agapito, for putting the film/documentary together, and for always having my back.

Thank you to Dr Simm, the psychiatric team at Winnipeg's Health Sciences Centre, the Addictions Foundation of Manitoba, and Tamarack Recovery Centre. Thank you to the Men's Resource Centre for giving me a safe space when I needed it most, and thank you to everyone who supported me through my 12 steps. Shout out to the special people in our men's group.

Last, but the furthest thing from least, my dearest Shannon. "Thank you" is not enough when it comes to you. You're my angel, my soul mate, and my best friend. You have loved me, and believed in me, and have been by my side since the day we met, never once giving up on me, even in the times you should have. No words can ever express my gratitude. You and Mitch have allowed me to be part of your family, and I'm proud to be a part of it.

If I forgot to thank anyone, my apologies. So many people have touched my life in positive ways, and if you're close to me, you know forgetfulness is part of my charm.

Always speak your truth, even if your voice shakes.
Sober straight edge soldier.
A life full of community service pays off with peace of mind.

CONTENTS

INTRODUCTION

Hi. I'm Roland.

You know, life has always seemed impossible for me.

I suffer from Post Traumatic Stress Disorder, the result of chronic abuse which began when I was a teenager. I would bet if anyone were to ask my principals, teachers, coaches, or family, they would all tell you the same thing: "Something wasn't right with Roland. We just didn't know what."

I went many years without help. My moods became uncontrollable. Fueled by alcohol and whatever drugs I could get my hands on, my seething anger boiled over and came out in the form of rage.

Today, I still feel as if I'm too damaged to make it in this world, but my bottom was so bad ... I can't go back.

I can't go back.

I am still conflicted about who to trust, and I consistently try to figure out who my real friends are. Thoughts that people are plotting behind my back or talking about me negatively run through my head when I think too much.

I'm nothing. I'm a nobody.

Shut up, brain.

I can stop that thought pattern by looking at reality. A lot of people love and care for me, and I have to believe those people can't be wrong. I must be worth it. I must be something.

Why couldn't anyone see the signs of what I was going through? Why didn't I tell anyone? It is my hope this book will provide some insight into the signs of abuse or neglect. Hopefully the words on these pages are a gateway. Hopefully my story can help prevent abuse before it happens. Hopefully my story helps readers get the courage to ask questions, or ask for help if needed. No matter what the problem is, no one should have to suffer in silence.

My name is Roland, and I'm an alcoholic. And an addict.

But most importantly, I'm a survivor.

This is my story.

DOWN FOR THE COUNT

CHAPTER 1

May 14, 2002

Everyone has left me. Again.

Where the fuck is everyone?

Where the fuck are the drugs?

I frantically search the hotel room. Is there anything left in this piece of foil? In that piece of foil? Nothing. There are a few half bottles of beer, and a part bottle of whiskey.

I take a few sips of the whiskey and chug one of the warm, open beers. Oh my God. What was that? Christ, it's a cigarette butt. I puke onto the floor and take another shot of whiskey to ease my stomach.

The loneliness is unbearable. Should I call Mom? Or should I call Shannon? I need to call Shannon, I miss her so much.

I call no one.

Where is everyone?

Thoughts of worthlessness wash over me, like a chant, playing over and over:

I'm no good.
I'm all alone.
Nobody loves me.
I can't do anything right.
I'm a loser.

Where are all my friends, and why did they leave me all alone in this room? They were all here for the past four days. Was it four days? I think it was? When did they leave? How long have I been here? Where can I get more booze and drugs? Jesus Christ, even that hooker is gone. She's my only avenue for drugs. Who else gives a fuck about a homeless and broke loser like me? No one.

Where are the drugs, for fuck's sake?

I'm no good.
I'm all alone.
Nobody loves me.
I can't do anything right.
I'm a loser.

Why did everyone leave?

If only I had a gun. I could blow my head off. I guess I could use the knives, but that would make too much of a mess. And if it doesn't kill me, I'll end up in the hospital.

Pointless.

Thoughts spiraling, each a left hook to the head.

The cops are coming to get me.
Bikers are coming to get me.
I miss Shannon.
I'm an idiot for losing Shannon.
No one loves me.
I'm worthless.

So much pain. Make this fucking shit stop.

My body is in agony. Years of hockey and fighting injuries have done me in. Fuck, when did I last eat? Four days ago? Five days? A week? Over the previous five months, I have smoked in excess of 150 thousand dollars of crack cocaine. Man, I wish I could find some crack. Did I check the foil? I think I checked the foil. I'll check it again.

My lips are chapped and bleeding, and my fingers are burnt and scabbed from lighting so many crack pipes. I hate myself.

God, I smell awful. I am disgusting.

I catch a glance of myself in the mirror. I'm a shadow of my former self, skin and bone, nowhere near my fighting weight. I have destroyed my life, it's unmanageable. I can't see any possible way I can be restored. I'm done.

My body is giving out, and giving up on me, just like everybody else.

Christ, I'm in such a hole financially. Should I get a job? Will that help? Can I fix it? Why am I thinking about this? I don't care.

Fuck. The dribble of alcohol is doing nothing. I hurt. All over. I need to be numb. Did I check the foil? I should check it again. Maybe I missed some residue, or a piece of crack. I'll check the foil.

Nothing.

I'll check it again to be sure.

Fuck you, foil. You let me down too.

The cops are coming to get me.
Bikers are coming to get me.
I miss Shannon.
I'm an idiot for losing Shannon.
No one loves me.
I'm worthless.

My eyes dart around the room. What's that yellow bottle? Oh. It's methadone. I heard it's like heroin. Have I taken heroin before? Maybe? I might have. That one time.

I need a way out of my head and my life.

Fuck, I'm alone.

They were all just going to hurt me anyway. I am better off on my own, and everyone is better off without me. Who wants a no good loser in their life? I am 31 years old, not even half a man, and I don't have enough money to even make a phone call. Who could love me? Oh my God! What happened to my life?

I look down at the bottle.

It's like heroin, they say.

I wonder how much is in this bottle? Enough to kill me?

I have fucked everything up so bad.

No one trusts me anymore. I tell people about my goals and dreams and I *see* them rolling their eyes. I know they're thinking, "Sure, sure Roland." I *know* they are thinking that.

I have lost all respect and dignity. Fuck, did I ever have respect or dignity?

I have crossed too many lines.

I know all of you hardcore "friends" are drinking and partying in the bar below. Do you even know I am up here?

I wish one of you would come through the door and help me.

Why won't one of you come up here and help me?

Fuck you.

I pace the room and peek out the windows like a paranoid crackhead. Oh my God. Am I a paranoid crackhead? I look under the door for shadows of the police coming, and listen for "the plan" to break the door down.

Yes. Paranoid crackhead. I don't care.

The cops are coming to get me.
Bikers are coming to get me.
I miss Shannon.
I'm an idiot for losing Shannon.

No one loves me.
I'm worthless.
Is there anything left in that foil?
Did I hear something?

Maybe one of the knives. Maybe that big hunting knife. I can run into a wall with it pointed at my chest. Or I could slit my throat. Or slash my wrists? Shit, that's pathetic. What if Mom or Shannon sees that mess? Fuck, who am I kidding. I'm too chicken.

Coward.

My chest is tight. Is my heart going to stop? Am I having a heart attack? Thank God if I am.

No such luck.

I peek out the window. What's that? Is that my friend's truck? What's that noise? Is someone here?

Nope. Just empty bottles and foils.

Are the foils empty? I'll check. Maybe there's a leftover crack rock.

Dammit.

I look out the window one more time. Shit. I am no more than three floors up. If I jump, it probably won't kill me. Legs broken, wheelchair. Fuck.

No.

Not that way.

I have to do things right.

I have to MAKE things right.

I put the yellow bottle down, strip off my clothes and climb into the shower. The water is a welcome respite from the pain. I dry off, dress, and leave the bathroom.

Things are going to change, Roland. Things are going to change.

I spin the cap off the yellow bottle and drink it down.
This should kill me. I hope it kills me.

As I climb onto the bed, my thoughts turn to Shannon and my son Jesse. They'll be okay, right? And then there's Mom. I hope she will be okay. My dad's dead, and my brother's a loser. Fuck, she's dealt with so much. How long has it been since I talked to Mom? Three months? Maybe four?

As I lie under the covers, I am so proud of myself. I am showered and dressed. When Mom sees me at the morgue, she won't be embarrassed.

I am okay with dying. For once in my life, nothing hurts anymore.

What the hell. Why am I thinking of the bouncer who kicked me out of a bar five years ago? He had been at a house party later that night, and my friend and I beat him so badly, we thought we killed him. I'm sorry. I'm sorry to you and to everyone I have ever hurt. If only I could do it over again. But it's too late. I hope you all hear this apology. Somehow.

It's all over now. I feel so relieved. So at peace. I'm not a religious man but God, please take my life, and please take care of Mom, Jesse and Shannon.

This bed is so comfortable.
I hope I never wake up.

CHAPTER 2

What the flying fuck is that?

Why is the bathroom door hitting me in the head? The fuck? How did I get here?

Why am on the bathroom floor with my head at the door and my feet by the toilet? Why can't I move? Am I paralyzed?

What is that smell? Jesus Christ, did I shit my pants? Holy fuck. I have shit my pants and pissed myself. Is that puke on my shirt?

Are you kidding me? I can't even kill myself properly. And I fucking shit my pants.

Another fail on my part.

I try to scream "Help me!" but the words won't come out.

Hours must have gone by. Hours? Really? What fucking time is it? What day is it? How long have I been lying here? Minutes? Seconds? I have no clue.

Why is this door banging me in the head when no one is here?

What the fuck? And then, it hits me. Like the bathroom door.

I am 31 years old and lying in my own shit. I have tried to kill myself. This. Is. My. Bottom. Get a grip, Roland.

GET A GRIP.

My poor mother, all she has gone through. My dad! I swear I just talked to him. How the fuck did I just talk to him?

My beautiful son Jesse. And Shannon. And my Uncle Dan holding our family together as he always does. What have I done? What have I done to them?

What the fuck do they think of me? Am I hallucinating?

What does this mean? Is this punishment for the crimes I committed? Thank God I was never caught as an adult. Fuck, was I ever lucky.

Wait. This is luck?

I see Shannon again. She's so pretty. I love her so much.

Is this a spiritual experience? Why didn't I die? I wanted to die. I want to die.

There must be a reason.

Right? There must be a reason? What fucking reasons? I'm a loser.

I am finally able to get up. The pain is back, but it's different. I strip off my clothes and put my underwear in the sink. I clean myself up.

My friend Colin once mentioned 12 step meetings. He had also said he had gone to the Health Sciences Centre for chemical withdrawal. Is this what I need?

Like I would know.

I make my way to the telephone and dial.

My mom answers.

"Mom, I'm sorry, but if you don't come get me, I'm dead. If you don't get here soon, I'm going to kill myself. I'm at the Norvilla Hotel and I'll be waiting in the lobby."

I am calm, but frantic. I do my best to clean up the traces of drug use in the room. I put on my pants and tuck my shirt, underwear, and drug evidence into a plastic bag. I open the door, look both ways to ensure all is clear, and make my way to the lobby.

I have no money to pay the bill, I hope they don't say anything. And then I see my mom's car.

I jump in, and tell her to take me to the hospital. She is already headed in that direction.

We travel in silence. I can tell Mom is devastated by the sight of me. She hands me a pack of cigarettes, drops me at the Emergency entrance, and tells me I am on my own.

So, this is tough love. I guess I have earned it. I have hurt her so much.

CHAPTER 3

I sat in the emergency waiting room for hours. The nurses and doctors didn't care that I was there. I was so sick and weak, surrounded by people who were nowhere near as sick as me. Twice a nurse asked what was happening and why I needed to see a doctor.

"I'm dying."

She didn't listen.

I couldn't believe it. In my head I screamed, "Do any of you know what the fuck I've been through? Why won't you help me?"

My thoughts wouldn't stop. "Should I take a run at the glass window or break my arm on the counter? WHAT WILL MAKE THEM SEE ME?"

I told the triage nurse if I didn't see a doctor right away, I would leave. And if I left, I would kill myself. Finally it sank in, and she took me to the back to see the doctor.

I told him what I'd gone through. Everything poured out, and finally someone listened. I was admitted to the addictions unit.

I was taken to a room and fed. I can't remember what I ate. A nurse came in and successfully put an IV in my arm, after others had struggled to find a vein. She patted my cheek and stroked my hair, and asked if I was okay.

And then the tears came.

I had not let myself feel anything real in years.

I told her I really needed to sleep. She told me I was safe, and I believed her.

When I woke up, I didn't know where I was, but slowly started to put things together. I had an IV in my arm, but it still wasn't clear where I was. What hospital was I at?

I asked a nurse. She said I was at the Health Sciences Centre.

"Am I okay?"

"Yes, you're fine. Would you like some food?"

"Yes, and some water."

A whole day passed as I alternated between sleeping and crying. And then I called my people: Mom, my friend Cris, my friend Monty, and finally, Shannon.

Monty came down with two packs of smokes, VHS movies, and clothes. A nurse came in and hooked my IV to a rolling carrier so Monty and I could go for a smoke.

The outside air felt good.

Beginning my new life felt good.

ROUND ONE

CHAPTER 4

I was born in 1971 in the Okanagan Valley, and the memories I have of my early childhood are, for the most part, good. Though honestly, I'm not sure if these are real memories, or incarnations of stories told to me through the years. I do know for certain I loved spending time with my father Maurice. I took pride in the fact that his middle name was Roland and my middle name was Maurice, and I wanted to be just like him. Dad was a structural iron worker and the four of us, Dad, Mom, and me and my older brother Jeff had a good life back then.

When I was around five years old, we moved to Gillam, Manitoba. My father worked in camps, and when he wasn't working, he'd take Jeff and me hunting or fishing. He was a tough man and I wanted his attention. I could always find trouble, and gravitated towards kids who were in the wrong crowd, so to speak.

I wanted to be like my father—in every way—so stealing a beer or two from him was common practice, long before I entered double digits in age.

I had no idea then that those early bottles of beer would lead to me developing a dependency on alcohol and drugs in an effort to "solve" my problems. At the time, I didn't realize I had problems.

I also began pinching cigarettes and lighters from my dad. One day, as I flicked a lighter in the bathroom, the wall went up in flames. Thankfully, no one was hurt. I was in more trouble than an eight-year-old could imagine, but wow, the fire was beautiful.

Back then, I thought friendship could be bought, so I would take money from my parents and buy candy to give my friends—it was a way to make them like me. And they did like the candy, so when there was no money to steal at home, I would steal directly from the store. The last time I lifted candy from that shop, the RCMP brought me home to two furious parents. My father insisted I return all the candy, and then tanned my butt.

But I wanted to be accepted by my peers, a group of children who, as I recall, had very similar home lives as me, and mischief was a part of our makeup, especially my makeup. Getting in trouble was a way to get attention—attention I wasn't getting elsewhere.

The fire in our bathroom and the petty theft in Gillam was just the beginning. When we moved to Winnipeg after a couple years in northern Manitoba, my ways didn't change. I gravitated to the same types of kids. I looked for trouble, and I found it.

We hadn't been in Winnipeg long when I stole some gasoline, set my school's field on fire, and had my first introduction to the Winnipeg Police. Yet another ride home in the back of a cruiser car to angry parents, followed by another tanned butt.

CHAPTER 5

My mother Marie always tried to keep things happy in our home. The fridge was always stocked with beer, and my parents often hosted gatherings for family and friends. My mom was (and still is) an amazing cook and she enjoyed feeding her boys and the stray kids we picked up in the neighbourhood.

My parents had us involved in community sports and attended all our games. Sports, especially hockey, gave us all a chance to meet people and make friends. Mom is very friendly, and my dad was a calm drunk who was very funny and likeable. As our family settled in in Winnipeg, my parents made many friends in our new neighbourhood.

As we got older, my parents spent more and more time at the local pubs, and I often had to seek them out at the local bar to get my allowance.

With no parents at home, our house became a regular hangout for my brother and his friends. As I got older, I became more and more uncomfortable around my brother, so I never really wanted to be home when he was there drinking with his pals.

My brother was different. I still can't put my finger on it, but he was never quite "right." He and his friends were the known troublemakers in the community—they were the dealers and sold joints at school. This brought him some popularity and notoriety, and made them think they were the shit. They would get drunk in my parents' basement and pick on me. Older siblings are supposed to do that, some might say, but this was not that. It went beyond the normal "older brother showing his kid brother the ropes."

Often, when my brother and friends took over the house, I'd escape. I'd roam the neighbourhood with kids like me, the kids whose parents weren't around. We partied and drank and soon realized we didn't need drugs to get high. We would hyperventilate, breathing in and out as fast as we could, and would chase each other around until we fell to the ground and passed out.

At 12, I lost my virginity at a house party. I was in seventh grade, and was the first kid in my group to have sex. I wore the label with pride, even though the sex itself was a truly awful experience.

Bush parties became a regular escape for me, with drinking, drugs, and sex. When Friday afternoon came, I did my chores and off I went. Our group realized if we sprayed Pam cooking spray in a bag and inhaled it we would get high. I stole a lot of Pam from our local store.

I stole from my parents so that I could buy beer and smokes for me and my friends. I knew Mom had a few places she hid money, so I'd help myself to her cash, or take my dad's change when he was passed out. I'd crawl slowly along the bedroom floor to get to Mom's purse or Dad's pockets while they slept. I figured since they were drunk, they wouldn't notice, not that I cared. I also took the car keys when they slept, tentatively taking the car around the block. By the time I was 12, I would take the car for hours at a time. I could hardly touch the gas pedals, and I would bring sweaters or something to sit on so I could see over the steering wheel. I would go pick up my friends late at night so we could party. I had a car, money and booze from my parents' fridge. I was the man, and it was on!

Whenever I had the chance to go drinking, that's exactly what I would do. By the time I was 13, blackout drinking and anger had become a regular part of my life. I would often wake up with dried blood on my knuckles and stains on my clothes with absolutely no clue about what happened the night before. My friends would fill me in.

But, I came by my love of fighting honestly. Boxing was a big deal in our family, and I grew up watching my Uncle Dan and cousin Doug in the ring. Seeing them and Donny Lalonde fight, I soon realized I wanted to be a boxer myself. I began going to the Pan Am Boxing Club and loved the masculine atmosphere of the gym.

My coach was named Ed. He was great. He pushed me hard, and finally, I earned the right to have a match. I was 13 years old, and was going to have a real bout in Brandon, Manitoba. Not only was I going to be able to fight, but I was also getting a weekend away. Only problem was Coach Ed couldn't make the trip, so a coach from another gym volunteered to chaperone the trip.

QUEER STANCE

CHAPTER 6

Traveling for the bout was very exciting, but something wasn't right. The coach who was taking us made the hair on my neck stand up every time he visited our gym. He seemed to go out of his way to talk to me, and when he did, I was uncomfortable. But I was a kid, what did I know? And this was my chance to fight.

On our first night in Brandon, I woke up in the dark hotel room to the feeling of someone touching my genitals.

"Shhhhhhhhh…shhhhh," came a whisper.

I looked down and saw the coach had my penis in his mouth. I was crippled with fear and lay still, but finally found the courage to push him away. He overpowered me, and all I could think to do was pretend to be asleep. He didn't stop. I pushed him off me again, which only made him mad. He grabbed my hands and forced me down. I felt paralyzed. "If only my dad were here," I thought to myself, "he'd beat the shit out of this guy."

I knew I had to get him off me. I began to make noise and finally others began stirring in the room. He finally climbed off me.

The next day, I pretended everything was okay. I stepped into the ring and pounded the shit out of my opponent. I received the win. Everyone was cheering for me and I loved it, but wanted desperately to get home. I couldn't wait to tell my dad about the match. He would be so proud of me. And he was, as was everyone else. I told no one about what happened in the hotel—I believed it was my fault. Did it mean I was gay because a man did that to me? They would blame me, and think I was gay.

I loved boxing but hated the thought of going back to the gym because he might be there. The few times I mustered the courage, I felt vulnerable and scared, so I told everyone I had headaches and quit.

CHAPTER 7

It probably sounds strange, but when they were sober, my brother's friends were fun to be around. When they were drunk, it was a different story. I became the focus of their attention. I was a punching bag for them, and when I tried to fight them off, they'd overpower me and tie me up. They'd slap me around a bit, or they'd burn me with the hot metal of a lighter. And then, they would make me touch them, and they would touch me. Eventually, a few of them moved on to raping me. The things they did to me (and what they made me do to them) are, to this day, unspeakable. I felt dirty and wanted to die.

My home wasn't safe, and I spent many nights at friends' houses. My mom never understood why. I was too ashamed to tell her I had been physically and sexually abused by six different males.

Thankfully I met Shannon. She gave me hope and she made me feel important. I think the only reason I even went to school was to see her. Shannon is, and always will be, the love of my life.

Shannon's family was everything I ever wanted. I loved her mother, Linda, and was enthralled with her dad, Roy, whom everyone called Herbie. Linda and Herbie split up shortly after I met Shannon, but they were still a family, and I was able to spend time with all of them. They were from a lineage of millionaires, having owned a chain of flooring stores and car dealerships. Everyone—aunts, uncles, grandparents and cousins—lived large, with cottages and yachts at Winnipeg Beach. They had beautiful show cars, mansions, and what seemed to be the high life. I desperately wanted to be part of that family and live that life. I am certain Shannon's family didn't like me at first because I had a pretty bad reputation. I kept trying though. I would clean up after lunch or supper, ask questions, and show interest. Eventually they accepted me, and to this day, they remain an important part of my life. If not for them, I am certain I would not be alive today. They had no idea what had happened to me. I kept up a good front. Shannon has since told me she had no idea I suffered so much.

CHAPTER 8

I pushed every memory as far down as I could, until the memories lay in my gut like a cesspool of rot. The pain was constant. I felt so alone and worthless, and not a day went by that I didn't want to die.

I took on the roles of hero and rebel, and would put myself at risk on a continuous basis. I needed to be noticed as something, *as someone*, important. I sought both approval and hatred, and I would do whatever I wanted, whenever I wanted, with no fear of consequences. No one cared about me anyway. I was just a worthless piece of crap, so, whatever, right?

But I lived by a code: never rat out your friends. If we were throwing rocks at houses, or buses, or even people, we'd run and scatter in different directions so that most of us could get away. When someone got caught, if they told who else was there, the consequences were swift. When I was questioned in the police car, and again in front of my parents, I never said a word. I understood the street code. You take one for the team, even if it's a criminal charge. We're all kids. It's not like they're going to do anything, right?

THE CUT MAN

CHAPTER 9

When you box, there's a guy in your corner who has the balls to cut your face to relieve swelling and pain. He tends to your wounds, and makes you feel better if only for a moment.

I learned if I cut or burned myself it would lessen the emotional turmoil inside. Like my brother and his friends used to do to me, I frequently flicked my lighter, heating up the metal end, and pressed it into my arm. For those few seconds I felt nothing but the burn, and oddly, happiness. Ironically, the result was my skin being singed with what looked like a happy face.

I would also cut myself in visible places on my arm. I would roll up my sleeves and sit next to my dad, hoping he would look at my wounds. I made sure I never cut too deep, because as much as I wanted to die, I didn't want to die. "Cut just enough to not die, Roland! Cut just enough so he asks what happened." He never asked.

And at night, I would scratch my skin so raw I bled. I would dig my nails deep into my skin so that when it scabbed up you could distinctly see an "s.w." Shannon's initials. I tagged myself to show my loyalty to her and in my mind, the scabs would show her and everyone else that she was my girl.

CHAPTER 10

My brother did have a good side, and sometimes he even protected me.

Our family was at a wedding. I was 13 years old, and somehow stole a bottle of whiskey from behind the bar. I drank the whole thing, and stumbled my way home to pass out, while my parents continued with the festivities. My brother knew what I'd done and headed home.

By the time he got home, I was pissed out of my brain. I went to sleep, and at some point in the night, woke up, loaded a shotgun, and aimed it at him as he slept. He woke up, grabbed the gun, and broke it. He could see I was in trouble. He put me on the handlebars of his bike, and sped to a nearby hospital.

He left me at the ER. My stomach was pumped, and I called Uncle Dan to take me home.

Mom Marie and Dad Maurice Vandal

VALLEY GARDENS
PEE WEE
TIER 3
B DIV CHAMPS
1983-84

Valley Gardens Seals Hockey Team

Young Roland watches boxing in excitement
while his hero uncle Dan Vandal signs autographs

Roland hockey pic in high school

Roland and Shannon, grad lovebirds

Roy (Herbie), Linda, Shannon, Roland,
Mom and Dad at our wedding

Roland holding baby Jesse Vandal

Convention Center, hometown heroes—
Roland vs Lee Laquette

Convention Center, hometown heroes—
Roland vs Lee Laquette with Dale, Jesse, Onalee and Donny

Roland HOW (Humans of Winnipeg) photoshoot

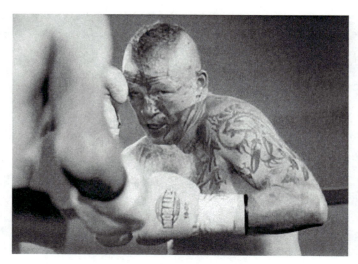

Roland pro boxing pic (*Winnipeg Free Press*)

Costa Rica with Undisputed World Champ Donny Lalonde

BOB AND WEAVE

CHAPTER 11

All through junior high I was bullied for what I wore by kids who were better off. I had the cheap jeans, and was called a welfare bum. I hated my parents for making me wear them. I hated my teachers, and I hated the principal Mr. Botting, but I had what I thought were a solid group of friends, and despite the bullying, I could exercise some power at school. I was a bit of an enigma. I was bullied myself, but I would float between teasing other kids for what *they* wore or how *they* looked, and sticking up for others I felt had been wronged. The "others" were kids like me, kids who didn't have perfect lives at home. As my friend Jennifer says, "We huddled together and were there for each other."

But fighting wasn't the only thing I did, and I was a frequent flyer at the Manitoba Youth Centre.

Stealing was easy, and every day or two, I went to a nearby shopping centre to stock up. Back then, cigarettes were out in the open in stores. I would load stuff in a shopping cart so the bottom was covered, load cartons of cigarettes on the undercarriage, and nonchalantly roll the cart out of the store. I'd steer the cart around the back of the building where my friends were patiently waiting for me. We would load up our jackets and take off. Cigarettes were our currency, and money was all that mattered.

A floorwalker busted me one time and brought me into the security office. I put on the waterworks and convinced security if they called the police, I'd be finished because my dad was a violent man who beat me every day. They bought my act and let me go. I felt larger than life! I one-upped the world! "Stupid fuckers,"

I thought to myself. "I'm the man and I'm way better than my stupid brother and his friends. Losers! I'll show them how good of a criminal I am!"

Not long after that, my friends and I did a break and enter on a house, and thought we had been successful. I went home and to bed, only to be awoken by flashlights pointed at my face. It was the police and they told me to slowly get out of bed and pull on my pants. I was searched and questioned, but I said nothing. I was handcuffed and taken to the nearest district and questioned for hours. I kept my silence. The cops told me the guys I'd been with had been busted and gave up my name. I didn't know if it was true, so I said nothing, and I took my charges like a solid mothafucka.

The hits kept coming. I broke into a house while the home-owners were sleeping, and then I broke into a convenience store. I was also charged with sexual assault, when the mother of one of my female friends walked in on four of us fooling around over the lunch hour.

CHAPTER 12

I felt disconnected and tormented at school. I was really happy to get out of junior high, and move on to high school. When I finished grade nine in 1986, I was happy to be away from Principal Botting. He was hard on me, and I certainly wasn't going to answer to him for anything. I kept getting suspended and sent home and I didn't ever want to be home. I was so glad to be out of his school.

September rolled around and that meant hunting and hockey season. I couldn't wait to start grade ten. It was going to be my year. It was scary walking into the high school the first day, but I was the man, and I didn't let it show. Sitting in class, I got called to the office. I got up, puffed out my chest and marched down to the office like a very important person, completely bulletproof. The secretary told me the principal wanted to see me and gestured for me to take a seat. I sat for about 20 minutes feeling annoyed and embarrassed as kids walked by and stared at me.

The door to the principal's office swung open, and out walked Mr. Botting. "What the fuck is going on? Why is he here?" I asked myself.

"Roland, come in," he said.

I sat down in the office, and there was an uncomfortable silence before he told me he was the school's new principal. I felt sick.

"I know all about your brother and his friends and what they did here, and I know you, Roland. They all dropped out and if that's what you want for your life that's your choice, but I know you and I feel you have the ability to be a success and graduate," he said.

"I'm not going to settle for any less. I talked to your hockey coach and every time you don't come to school or get in trouble, your hockey coach is going to bench you. Don't even think of not passing. Do you understand?"

My stomach was churning.

"Furthermore, do you see that desk in the corner? That's yours. If I have to suspend you for anything, you'll serve it here, in my office, and you'll do your school work. Is that clear to you, Roland?"

I couldn't say a word. I realized he had my number and I had to keep my shit together. Shannon wouldn't want to date a drop-out loser, and if I couldn't play hockey? And I really didn't want to be like my brother and his friends. They were all dope smoking wannabes whose main goal was to be on welfare. I nodded, and left the office.

"Who does he think he is," I thought as I walked back to class. "I am going to show everyone I'm better. I'm going to graduate and prove everyone who thinks I'm like my brother wrong."

CHAPTER 13

I took air conditioning and refrigeration in high school, because that's what my brother failed at. I was going to do the same and succeed. Whatever he did I was going to do better. Thought he was tough in hockey and on the street? Well I'm tougher. He made money? I'm going to make more. He flunked out? I'm going to graduate.

I was able to get passing grades in high school without really trying. My friend Marcel, who was someone I once got in a fist fight with, was a smart guy who knew how to make legit money. He was a few years older than me, and worked as a gas station manager. I asked him for a job and he hooked me up. But I wanted more and I was going to get it.

I had started toying around with selling pot in grade nine. Every night I would sit down and roll a half ounce in joints and sell them to the kids I hung out with. Once I hit high school I really stepped up my run at the drug-dealing world. I had jobs, sold drugs, and always had money in my pocket. I worked hard at the jobs I had, and I sold as much dope as I could in the hopes I could save money and buy myself a car. If I did that, my dad would be proud of me for being so successful at a young age. Just a smile or nod from him drove me to do better. I loved my dad so much, but I hated him for being a drunk. He was such a strong man, but when it came to him and his alcohol, it owned him and came before everything, including me and the rest of our family.

By 16, I had my driver's licence and I convinced my grandparents to lend me $5000 so I could buy a truck. In theory, I would pay my grandparents back from the money I was making. I was so proud of that truck, and I felt, for once, on top of the world. I could go hunting or camping whenever I wanted, and I could squire Shannon around as much as she needed. I had freedom.

THROWING IN
THE TOWEL

CHAPTER 14

At 16 I was at a friend's house, smoking pot with a bunch of kids when the door came crashing down. Police stormed the house with guns drawn and I found myself in the middle of a drug raid. The dogs in the house were going crazy while the cops were yelling, "Get on the floor."

When the cops noticed a pellet gun on the table, the scene escalated and became frantic. I wasn't scared, and kept telling myself to not say a thing. We were all placed in separate rooms. I was forced face down on the floor, handcuffed, and a towel was placed over my head while the police searched the house. I lay there for what seemed like hours before the cops finally questioned me. They had found hash and mushrooms in the house, as well as some pot and 16 grams of hash in my truck.

I realized no one had owned up to the drugs found in the home, and since I was already going down for the drugs in my truck, I told the cops the drugs in the house were mine. It was the right thing to do, and it was my fucking chance to prove to people how worthy I was. I would prove to my dad and my brother and his asshole friends I was a man. I knew my parents were going to freak out, but I knew my dad would also be proud of me for taking the hit for my friends. He would realize how much more solid I was than my brother. My dad would know I was worth *something*. The world would know I was something. "Fuck anyone who tries to touch me or hurt me again," I thought on the way to the Youth Centre, "Embarrass me one more fucking time and I'll shoot you."

I was charged with possession and didn't care. I knew the Young Offenders Act would protect me. The older kids, the 18-year-olds, they would have been charged as adults. I took all the charges like a man.

After I was released, people respected me. I was "solid," and walked around with my chest puffed out. I was larger than life. I wasn't a rat. Fuck, I was a hero! I was the man!

Even though I hated my brother and his friends, it's clear I was attracted to the chaos of their lifestyle. The drugs. The crime. The perceived power. I wanted all of it, and deep down I desperately wanted their approval. I was going to show them how important and powerful I was. I was going to do everything they did, but bigger and better. They couldn't hurt me anymore, and fuck them if they tried.

IN MY CORNER

CHAPTER 15

My dog Baron was a beautiful black Labrador retriever, and I loved spending time with him. When I cried myself to sleep he would come and put his head on my neck and console me. Sometimes, he'd nuzzle his nose under my arm, and move my arm out of the way to maneuver his way under the covers.

That dog meant everything to me. Nothing made me happier than packing Baron into my truck and heading out to Libau Marsh or the Whiteshell to hunt. He was a smart dog, and won ribbons in hunting competitions.

Hunting is an all-day experience, and the best part of hunting was the time Baron and I spent together. As we'd wait for the sun to rise, sitting among the dew-covered cattails and swamp grass, Baron would shake with excitement. He knew what was coming.

In the distance, geese would rise and fly across the horizon, and as the birds came into range of my shotgun, Baron's eyes would light up.

I'd pull the trigger and "boom!" Baron would swim towards the bird, barreling through the thin layer of ice.

"Good boy, Baron," I'd say, offering praise to my best friend, when he returned with the bird.

Baron gave me hope. Baron would never hurt me. He understood loyalty. He loved me, and it was unconditional. When things were really bad at home, I would sometimes grab a blanket and take Baron to go sleep in the park across the street.

ROLLING WITH THE PUNCHES

CHAPTER 16

My relationship with Shannon became an obsession. Thoughts of living without her were crippling and devastating. Shannon owned me, and I wanted and needed her and her family so desperately. I did anything for her attention and if anyone threatened my emotional security around her, the fight was on. I was desperate, insecure, jealous, needy, and clingy when it came to Shannon and her family because I felt safe under Linda's roof. The rare times I did sleep at home, I would put a knife in the door to block people from coming in, or I'd set up beer bottles behind the door so if someone came in I would hear them.

My brain was so messed up, and I acted out in all sorts of ways. I needed to be needed and I would pretty much do anything for affirmation. I hated myself. I hated how I felt, and I hated my pathetic life. The only times I felt good about myself was when I was with Shannon, with Baron, when I was drunk, or when I was fighting.

Drinking whiskey helped me muster up the courage to be out and be social. People thought I was outgoing and a fun guy, but it was the booze, and the real "magic" happened when I was four or five drinks into the night. With that much liquor in me, I would put the crosshairs on someone around me. I would taunt and antagonize them, pushing for a fight. If I couldn't get a fight going, I'd punch holes in walls or destroy property. I wanted people to fear me. Fear, in my mind, equaled respect. My friends would egg me on.

CHAPTER 17

Hockey was a great release for me because I could take my aggression out on the ice. I wasn't a great puck handler, but I was a fast skater full of aggression with a decent slap shot. I had the hardest body check and something to prove, and that often resulted in my riding the bench or getting suspended, which is exactly happened during a game against St. John's-Ravenscourt. I took a penalty. I chipped at the referees, who threw me out of the game. As I left the ice, I ran across the concrete on my blades, throwing my gloves and helmet off in an attempt to fight the fans. My coach was forgiving, but I was called in front of the hockey commission and handed a four-game suspension.

My coaches Al, Bill, and Tim had a profound impact on me. They knew there were kids like me who needed guidance and discipline. If we weren't at practice, Bill would go to our houses. If we weren't at home, he'd take our equipment, put it in his truck, and look for us. Once he stormed into the food court at a shopping mall where we were trying to impress some girls. He was an ex-army guy, and when we saw him coming, we knew the gig was up. "Get the fuck in my truck!" he said, right in front of all the girls. And we did. It didn't matter how cold it was outside, he made us practice. He made us become a team.

All my buddies were great hockey players and I always wanted to play in the better leagues. The tier system leagues were expensive, and my parents wouldn't have been able to afford the fees, so I did what I could to sabotage any chance of me making those teams. But the reality was my heart was bigger than my skill level. My aggression was bigger than everything.

As much as I loved hockey, I hated changing in the change room with everyone. I would put my jock on under my clothes and or put my bottom half of equipment on before I went to practice. I was ashamed and scared.

When I got angry during games, I would cry and embarrass myself. Being embarrassed would cause me to get angrier to the point of anger blackouts. At one game, the other team's fans were taunting my team. I flipped out and skated up to the boards yelling at the hecklers. Fuming with rage, I hurled my stick, as if it were a spear, into the stands! It hit the wall in between two fans, and the ice broke out in chaos. Thrown out of the game, I trashed the dressing room.

Undeniably, the best part of hockey was the feeling I would get when I'd see Shannon in the stands. She'd be in a white fur coat, with fur mitts to match. Her hair was done and she was the most beautiful girl there. I'd feel amazing, knowing she was there to watch me.

When Al stopped coaching our team, it wasn't the same. After a half season, the players all quit. In the fall, I took it upon myself to rally a few of my teammates to beg Al to come back. He said, "Well, boys, if you get the team together I'll coach one more year." And so we did. By then, injuries were already taking their toll on me, and I knew it would be my last year playing. But 30 years later, I'm proud to say I still call Al a friend.

THE UNDERCARD

CHAPTER 18

When grade 12 rolled around, I set my sights on graduating. My buddies Roman and Quinn had similar home lives, and we were in the same classes, doing what we could to grind out our success. Quinn said he was going to take a fifth-class power engineering course that was offered on Saturdays. So I followed suit and signed up.

Roman and Quinn were so much like me. They had reputations and were tough, but more importantly they were loyal. They protected me from myself. I realized that I had enough credits to graduate midway through the school year. Here I was at 17, a high school graduate with a fifth-class power engineering certificate. I started working at an autobody shop, and could tell my mom and dad were proud of me. Mom gave me an I.O.U. for a set of golf clubs. It was the thought that counted most.

Mr. Botting was proud of me too, and I was proud I hadn't let him down by failing. He had advocated to keep me in school after I threatened a teacher who I felt embarrassed me in class. I didn't realize it then, but Mr. Botting was one of the first professionals who saw something in me, and wanted me to succeed. I'll never forget those people who were patient enough to talk to me. He clearly knew something was wrong, and without him and other educators giving me a safe place, I don't know where I'd be today. I wish I would have told him then what had happened to me.

CHAPTER 19

Early graduation afforded me the time to hang with some older guys from the neighbourhood who were known to be in biker gangs. My reputation as a solid guy who wasn't a rat allowed me to hover around that life without actually becoming a gang member. As with Shannon and her family, these guys made me feel safe and protected.

Just being affiliated with the guys got me a lot of respect. Here I was 17 years old and going to the bar with them. I was stoked. These guys were cool, and people knew who they were dealing with. They all had mechanic shops, and the shops became our party spots before and after the bar. I looked up to my childhood buddy Ken (name changed), who had risen through the ranks of an international biker gang, and was the leader of its Manitoba chapter.

I pulled away from my hockey friends because I believed I somehow had to surpass my brother's reputation. I wanted to be tougher than him, and stronger than him, and prove to everyone I was fearless.

I always felt I needed to up the ante and be crazier than everyone else. People were going to know that this 5'7", 140-pound kid had the biggest balls around, and there was no fucking around with me unless you wanted to get shit-kicked. Look at me the wrong way? I'll fight you. Dare say something out of line? You're going down. I was always ready to fight.

After the bar one night, I was back at my parents' house. My brother was with his buddies, and Dad was passed out at the kitchen table. My brother was bragging about beefing it out at the bar, and next thing we know, a group of guys start trying to kick in the door. My mom came running to the basement, terrified. I went upstairs with my mom, and yelled at everyone to get help. The door came in and flew directly into my mom, hurling her backwards. As she was falling back, a big guy punched her in the face. My brother and his friends began brawling with these guys in our house, and finally my dad woke up and lost his shit. The fight spilled into our backyard, and then into the back lane, and I can steal hear my mother's screams. I was happy my dad was up. The Vandal men were going to handle this. When I went outside to fight for my family, my dad yelled at me to go back in the house. I sat crouched down in the door, looking outside. My brother appeared with a shotgun, and was pointing it, ready to shoot. Dad grabbed the gun and threw it in the house. Finally, the guys ran back to their vehicle and raced off. The police came and my dad sent me to my room. I sat listening at the door, hoping my mom was okay. I couldn't make out what the police were saying, so I climbed into bed and cried.

GLASS JAW

CHAPTER 20

I don't think I really liked the violence, but I loved the excitement of bar brawls, and the attention I'd get after a good night of fighting. One night, my buddies and I were at a local bar, playing pool and downing drinks when a brawl broke out. The lights came up, and the DJ said over the PA system, "Everyone who doesn't want to be here leave now!" Some folks scurried out, but the brawl continued. Pool cues were flying, people were knocked out and then the whole brawl carried out into the parking lot. Of course I was right in the middle. I squared off in a fighting stance against a big biker dude. It was the middle of winter and I was juiced out of my mind. People were cheering me on, and we threw a few punches at each other. Then I went for the tackle. I always liked fighting on the ground because I could get mean. I slipped and fell on all fours, and felt a steel-toed boot hit me square in the face. I saw stars and watched blood splatter from my mouth the ground. I knew I was hurt bad. I don't know how much time passed before one of my buddies came over and picked me up off the ground. I might have passed out. I was barely able to walk, but my friend helped me down a back lane to a man lying on the ground. It was the guy I'd been fighting, the one who had kicked me in the face. I could taste the blood in my mouth, and got angry. The anger seemed to sober me up, and I got more stable as we walked towards him.

"We got him. Give him a kick, Rolly," was all the encouragement I needed, and I hauled off and booted him in the face.

The force of kicking him made me stumble. My friend grabbed me by the arm and steadied me, then sat me down on the curb. I was in a lot of pain, and felt something hanging in my mouth. I felt dizzy.

"Roland, let's see in your mouth," my friend said. I told him I was fine, and to leave me alone. He persisted and took a good look at me. "Bro, you gotta get to the hospital right now."

Another of my buddies gave me a ride, while another followed in my truck. I asked to go to Shannon's house. I pounded on her front door, and her mom answered. I saw Shannon standing at the top of the stairs, and asked to see her. Linda was shocked at the sight of me. I was covered in blood. I could hear Shannon telling her mom she didn't want to see me. Finally she yelled, "Leave, Roland! Get out of here," but Linda took pity on me and invited me in. She looked in my mouth and told me that I had to go to the hospital. She called Shannon over. Shannon gave me a tentative hug, but I could tell how angry and disappointed she was. I couldn't get the look on her face out of my mind all the way to the hospital.

My upper jaw was severely broken and would have to be reset. My mom was called, and my Uncle Dan came to be with me. The doctor and a team of nurses positioned themselves all around me and explained what they were doing. The doctor was behind me holding my head, while nurses and other staff held my arms, shoulders, knees, legs and feet. They asked me to hold on and put something deep in my mouth so that I couldn't bite down on the doctor's fingers. Memories of being held down by my brother and his friends came rushing back, and sheer panic overtook me. When the doctor asked if I was ready, my mind said "no" but I nodded anyway. He put his two fingers in my mouth and pulled my teeth and jaw back into place. The pain was like nothing I've ever felt. A nurse sat me up and suctioned the blood out of my mouth. Shortly after, my mouth was frozen and wired shut. I don't remember a whole lot from the days that followed, other than calling Shannon. She was very kind to me, but I knew she was angry with the whole situation. I asked her if I could stay at her place when I was released from the hospital.

Her mom made a bed on the couch and took good care of me. I was officially her fourth kid.

HOMETOWN COOKING

CHAPTER 21

Shannon's cousin Shawn and I began to hang out a lot more. At the same time, my friend Marcel let me know he could get me a job at a flooring company. Shannon's whole family was in the flooring industry and I knew if I could get the flooring skills, I'd really be a part a better of her family. I met the owners and they were really good people. It was a win-win situation.

My days involved going to work, then to the bar, a fight, then an hour or two of sleep, and repeat. Shawn let me know his parents, Wayne and Judy, and his two brothers were moving to BC. Shawn was going to stay in Winnipeg.

Shannon's dad, Herbie, eventually made his way to BC too. He started a flooring business with Wayne, and when Shawn decided to move to BC in 1990, I decided I was going to head west too, just as my father had done so many years ago. I loved my mom and dad, and I loved my city, but I always felt I needed to get out of Winnipeg. Leaving would help me change my life. I'd have a fresh start.

After a send-off party at a bar, my buddy Brad and I packed up all of our belongings and started driving. Once we hit the outskirts of Winnipeg, I smiled. I was finally out. Finally free of everything. "Fuck you," I yelled to everyone as the city faded behind me. We drove straight through, drinking the whole time.

I was determined to build a life for me and Shannon on the coast. I had experience in the flooring industry, and my plan was to work for Shannon's family, and eventually convince Shannon to join me in BC.

I moved in with Wayne and Judy, and started working at the flooring company. I was away from the violence, and the daily partying. I talked to Shannon on a regular basis. After about five months in BC, my habitual drinking returned, and was becoming unmanageable. I would drink too much and get searing headaches. But it didn't stop me—I would do the same thing the next day.

One night I was in a bar in Port Coquitlam. I'd drunk a fair bit, and put myself in the middle of someone else's beef. I squared off with a guy. As I threw a punch, it sunk into my head that this was none of my business. I realized the police were probably on their way. I ran off and hid in my car. Peering through the window, I could see flashing lights. After that, things are pretty fuzzy.

The next morning, Wayne and Judy woke me in a panic.

"Roland, what the hell happened?" asked Wayne, as he shook me awake.

I had no idea what they were talking about. They took me outside. My car had huge scrapes down the driver's side and two flat tires. I had a vague recollection of hitting a meridian wall on the way home.

I remembered the fight, and realized I needed to watch my attitude in Vancouver. I didn't have twenty guys behind me, backing me up.

CHAPTER 22

I finally convinced Shannon to move out to BC. Shannon moved in with her dad and got a job. We were together again and I loved her, but I sure didn't show it. She spent evenings alone while I was partying it up.

I knew after a few months she wasn't happy. I thought I could keep her in BC if I asked her to marry me. I went to her father and asked for his permission and approval.

I planned the engagement and took Shannon to a restaurant on top of Grouse Mountain. When we got to the restaurant, I slid the ring to the host so it could be brought out with our food. Shannon and I sat at a table overlooking the mountains and Vancouver's lights. I was nervous, but excited. The food came and all the staff were peeking their heads around the corners. The ring was sitting on the tray and was put in front of Shannon. I got on one knee.

"Shannon, I've loved you since we were twelve years old and I want to spend the rest of my life with you. You are the best person I've ever met. Will you marry me?"

The whole restaurant was quiet and Shannon quietly said "yes." People applauded. I hadn't felt that much joy before.

We left the restaurant with smiles pasted on our faces. I was ecstatic she said yes, but reality set in. I had no sustainable plan past that point except to party.

Shannon tried to build a life in Vancouver, and would take the train to work every day. Me? I went to work, and then partied and drank. I didn't give her the attention she deserved.

"Roland, I need to talk to you," she said one day. "I love you but I can't do this anymore. I'm going home, back to Winnipeg." And the weirdest thing happened. I felt relieved. Shannon got in the way of my drinking.

Once Shannon left BC, I kept partying. We'd talk on occasion, and we were technically still engaged. She was working and having a good time back in Winnipeg. Friends told me one of my buddies was hitting on Shannon since I wasn't around.

My mind raced. She was moving on! She didn't need me. Fuck my friend, moving in on my girl. I had to get back to Winnipeg.

I talked to Wayne and told him I was going back to Manitoba. I rented a U-Haul, packed up everything, and thanked Shannon's family for helping me. It was tough to say goodbye, but I had to get to Shannon.

I drove straight through, only stopping to fuel up. I didn't eat, and peed in empty bottles. I had nothing on my mind but Shannon and my so-called friend who was trying to take her away from me.

I went straight to Shannon. Seeing her, and knowing what my friend had done, I made a few calls to find out where my friends were. They were at a social. I loaded a shotgun and threw it in my trunk. I was furious and ready to go. Word had spread that I was back, and that I had business to take care of.

I stormed into the social hall in an absolute frenzy. I scanned the room and saw my friends, friends who hadn't tried to take my girl from me.

"Where the fuck is Roman?" I asked them. "Hiding?"

He wasn't there.

A friend offered me a drink, and I calmed down. People welcomed me back, and I was kind of relieved I didn't have to fight my friend. But more drinks flowed, and my anger bubbled up. Roman, it turns out, was at a bar not too far away.

I saw him immediately. I was going to have it out with him, but by the time I crossed the bar, I was exhausted. He agreed to go outside and talk. Once we got outside, Roman grabbed and hugged me. After two days with no sleep, I broke. I sobbed on his shoulder as Roman patted the back of my head and my back.

Once I pulled myself together, we sat on the curb together, silent. We shared a couple of smokes, and went back inside together. It was over.

I went home and passed out for two days straight.

CHAPTER 23

Nothing, it seemed, had changed in the year I was gone. My dad was still at the kitchen table surrounded by empty beer bottles. Mom was on edge, trying to keep things together. And there I was, unemployed and broke, back in their basement. I was a failure.

My father barely spoke. I'd been away a year, and all he could say to me was "hello."

It killed me to see him so broken, he looked frail and ill. I wanted to shake him and say, "Dad, look at you! You are dying. Can't you see what you're doing to yourself? What you're doing to us?" But I was taught to never be disrespectful to my father. Instead, I took it out on my mom, which made things worse. I was as angry at her as I was at my dad.

What the hell I was thinking coming back to this? The only good thing that had happened in the past year was my brother had moved out of my parents' house. The pool table I had bought had been completely destroyed by my brother and his friends while I was gone.

My mom was so busy taking care of my dad she'd given up on taking care of the house. The only time the house got cleaned was if my grandma was coming over.

After a few weeks, I called Shannon. "I can't stay here, I can't live in this disaster," I said.

It was August 1991. My buddy Marcel helped me pick up some flooring work, and I'd got back into the drug dealing business. I rarely went home and stayed at Shannon's mom's house most of the time. Shannon and her mom had moved in with

Mr. Wall, Linda's partner. So I'd work, get drunk, drive to their place, and repeat it the next day.

I'd beg Shannon to come party with me, but she was ready to grow up, and didn't want to be around my friends, let alone me, with all the drinking and violence. I couldn't blame her, but I completely blamed her, and would start fight after fight.

Shannon didn't want that life. She always worked hard and wanted to succeed. I wanted to succeed too, and I worked hard, but I worked hard to succeed to get enough money for booze and drugs. I wanted to be with Shannon, but wasn't willing to grow up.

After a night of partying I went back to Shannon's and drunkenly convinced her to sleep with me. She had chosen abstinence, but I talked a good game. Soon after, Shannon told me she was pregnant, so we moved up our wedding date.

We were 21, and the celebration began. We had so much attention, and I felt affirmation because I had gotten Shannon pregnant. I was the shit. I was getting married, with a baby on the way. But truthfully I didn't want to be tied down. I wanted Shannon, but I wanted my party life more. Nonetheless, we moved into an apartment together and began planning the wedding. I kept partying as her pregnancy progressed, and was rarely home.

I was scared shitless.

Our wedding day came. I woke up feeling very overwhelmed, so I had a few drinks to soothe myself. It was a really beautiful wedding, poolside, Hawaiian style, at a local hotel. Once the ceremony was over the party was on. Shannon was disgusted by how much my friends and I were drinking, and went alone to our hotel room while I partied with my friends. Full of booze and cocaine, I staggered into our room in the wee hours of the morning.

COUNTERPUNCH

CHAPTER 24

As much as I loved Shannon, I hated being married. I hated having responsibility.

I'd party after work and Shannon would spend nights at home pregnant and alone, or she'd go stay with her mom. I didn't care. The domesticated, "boring" life wasn't gonna tie me down. I was Roland Fucking Vandal.

Thoughts of being a father would make my chest feel like it was going to explode. I couldn't pull together a rational thought. If I couldn't make decisions about shopping, how on earth would I be able to make decisions as a husband and father? It was easier to party with my buddies at their shops than to think about that, and I knew Shannon would "understand." Hours into the night, I'd call Shannon and ask her to meet me at the bar, and she would always say no, and ask me to come home.

My friends were my priority. Booze was a priority. When I was home with Shannon, we barely spoke, and I knew why. I consistently let her down. But I'd pick a fight with her so I could storm out and meet my friends. I thought I was content when I was with my friends, but really, I was only content knowing that my next drink was right within my reach.

CHAPTER 25

Things were so rough—I was gone so much—that Shannon got me a pager so she'd be able to find me when she went into labour.

I don't think Shannon worried too much about me when I was away from her. She knew the guys I was with were solid, and she knew they were all looking out for me. I know Shannon hated my drinking, and I know she hated my selling drugs, but she knew that I was as safe as I could be.

The baby was coming soon, so Shannon and I bought a house, and got the nursery ready. Not long after we'd settled into our new home, Shannon's water broke and we rushed to the hospital. Her mom and I stayed by her side the whole time. I couldn't stand seeing her in so much pain. I did my best to be supportive, pulling hair off her face, and feeding her ice chips. I don't know how supportive she thought I was, especially when I ordered a pizza and sat eating it in front of her.

They'd tried two epidurals, and kept missing. I yelled at the doctor, and was promptly told if I didn't calm down I'd have to leave. They tried again, but it didn't take. I did my best, rubbing her back and stroking her hair. At that moment, I would have done anything I could to take Shannon's pain away.

Finally, it was time to push, and I wasn't ready for what I saw. Shannon was a warrior, and I've never felt so proud as when the doctor exclaimed, "It's a boy!"

Our son Jesse Roland Vandal was finally here.

When I held him in my arms, I was consumed with thoughts of my past. How is a fuckup like me going to ever amount to any type of father?

I promptly left the hospital to celebrate with my buddies.

CHAPTER 26

My father loved Jesse more than anything. When he would see my son, his eyes would light up. I hadn't seen my dad look so happy in years. Dad knew I was fucking things up. During one visit, he sat me down. "Don't let Shannon go. Be a man. Be a father, Roland," he said.

But my dad didn't know. He didn't know that sometimes when I held my son memories of abuse would flood over me. He didn't know that every time I was near Jesse I couldn't shake the thoughts of what a terrible father I would be.

Smoking pot didn't help the situation. I thought it would relax me so that I could deal with being a father. Instead, it made me climb deeper into myself. I took on more work, and did anything I could to not be at home. At home, one thought consumed me: "You're no good, Roland. You're a loser. Who are you trying to kid?" When there was no work to be had, I'd park a few blocks from home listening to music, waiting for my friends to be ready to party.

I hid a lot of my income from Shannon so I'd have more money to spend on booze and drugs. I did a lot of under-the-table work, so she had no idea what I was earning. I could tell Shannon was getting tired of me and my exploits. If there was an award for worst father and husband, I would have won it.

I tried. I tried to connect with my son. I loved him, but the thoughts of being a functional father—a functional person—were beyond frightening. Looking at my son, I felt pain. Of course there were some special moments, the ones you put in the baby book, but I missed so many good times because I couldn't shake the memories of my past.

Shannon still had no idea what I'd gone through as a kid, and I had no intention of telling her. She'd think I was a monster. She'd know I didn't deserve her.

I was so worried that I was going to hurt Jesse. "What if? Why? Why me? Why six people? Am I an abuser too?"

I couldn't bear the thought I might harm Jesse.

After a year of me playing house, Shannon sat me down and told me she was taking Jesse and leaving.

I was relieved. Shannon and Jesse leaving meant I could have a really rocking pity party with my friends.

POUND FOR POUND

CHAPTER 27

I spent two weeks drinking and doing coke after Shannon and Jesse left. I decided it was time to tell my parents what had happened.

I never drank with my dad, but grabbed a beer out of the fridge and sat across from him. He was silent. As we finished our drinks, I broke down and told him Shannon had left me. I could see the disappointment in his eyes. I went to grab another beer.

"Leave that beer where it is and sit the fuck down!" he said. My dad never talked that way, especially in front of my mom.

"What happened?" he asked.

I told him Shannon and I had been fighting the last few months, how unreasonable she was, how hard I worked, how much I loved Shannon and Jesse. He was furious with me, so furious I thought he was going to hit me. He saw right through my lies and omissions, and told me to get the fuck out of his house.

I went back to my empty house. I had a couch and a TV, and little else. I plopped down on the couch and cried. I knew the only way to fix things was to be gone.

"If I run through the picture window, will it kill me?" My luck, I'd end up disfigured or as a vegetable. What about my knives? What about my guns?

No option seemed right, except getting drunk. So I called my buddies, and started the night.

CHAPTER 28

Free from marriage and the burden of being a father, my gang involvement grew. The best people I knew were bikers, and I wanted that life. I wanted that respect. I was going to get a patch in a gang if it killed me.

With connections to a couple of bike gangs, I was able to up my drug-dealing game. In my mind, dealing drugs was the best way to succeed and make money, so I started selling small quantities of cocaine at local bars. I carried sawed-off pool cues in my truck, and I had sawed-off shotguns hidden at different locations if I ever needed them.

I hadn't done much cocaine in my life—my brother had introduced me to coke a few years before—but I knew how great it was. The highs were fantastic, but I didn't have the cash to be a habitual user. The beauty of selling coke was having a personal supply that I didn't have to pay for. I quickly learned that I could drink massive amounts of alcohol and if I did a line of cocaine, it would sober me up. This became my daily routine.

In my head I was rising up the ranks in the biker community. We travelled in packs to the bars, with assorted baseball bats and golf clubs filling the trunks of our cars. We were always ready for a fight.

My house became a party house, and was a great place to cut cocaine. After a night of partying at the bar or my house, I'd deliver coke around the city, and sleep when I wasn't doing a flooring job. I could barely pay my bills. My money was going to cocaine and alcohol.

We were at a local bar when a fight broke out and spilled into the parking lot when a bouncer kicked us out. The fight was nothing new, it was the same as all the others. Our bats came out, and we cleaned house. There's a certain sound that's made when someone gets hit with a bat.

People were sprawled on the ground, and there were screams from girlfriends watching their boyfriends get hurt. The police came and as usual, no one spoke a word. We left, and headed to a party.

Twenty of us walked into the house, and who do we see? None other than the bouncer who kicked us out of the bar earlier. I locked eyes on him and nodded at my friend Army. As the night went on, things were escalating. A fight broke out, and the bouncer went outside with one of my buddies. They squared off, the hockey sticks and bats came out, and we were in and an all-out rumble. The bouncer was knocked out cold, and we started stomping him and kicking him in the head. I could hear his head bounce off the concrete. You never forget that sound. Over and over Army and I booted him in the head until we heard, "Okay you little fuckers, enough!" My childhood friend Ken had spoken, and when he spoke, no one argued.

We'd injured the bouncer so brutally, we thought we had killed him. Finally, he got up and staggered around looking to fight someone. "Shut the fuck up, buddy. Haven't you had enough?" someone said.

When he went back in the house, we left.

CAUGHT COLD

CHAPTER 29

I was approached by a biker associate and asked to convert my basement into a marijuana grow operation. I agreed to a percentage of the yield and set up shop. I was told me to keep my mouth shut, and not have anyone over, but I didn't listen. My house was still party central, and I was only slightly worried the police would bust me.

I only kept Shannon and Jesse away. My house reeked of marijuana, so I made excuses to not see them. I was so miserable without Shannon and Jesse, but I couldn't bear the thought of them near me. I didn't deserve them, and they sure as hell didn't deserve the punishment of being around me.

I would drink constantly, and sober myself awake with cocaine, barely making it to work most days. I started frequenting the local biker clubhouses and secret booze cans. My cocaine sales were taking off and I started getting larger quantities of drugs at my request.

Ken knew everything, and he was worried about what I was doing. He sat me down to let me know that I was a beacon for the cops. He knew I was running a grow op for another gang, and that I was not acting responsibly.

"Get your shit together, Roland. You're a fucking heat magnet. I see cops on the street around here all the time. Are you fucking stupid?" he asked.

Yes. I was that fucking stupid.

"Shit. He's right," I realized. I was a really horrible drug dealer and grow operator. People knew what I was doing, and I began to worry constantly. Paranoia crept in: either the police were coming or I was going to get home invaded from people who robbed grow ops. "As long as you make it a little bit longer, just enough to crop out, you'll make enough money to catch up on your bills and drug debts," I'd tell myself. "Just be smarter."

My brother started to show up at my house to party. I knew I needed to smarten up, keep the partying at bay until the crop came in, but he'd given me my first taste of cocaine, and I felt obligated in a sense.

One night, after everyone but my brother and his friends had left, they disappeared into my bedroom. I pounded on the door. "What the fuck are you doing in there?"

They came out and we all sat in the living room and drank. I said, "What the fuck? What were you guys doing?"

My brother went back to my bedroom and emerged with a plastic bag. He opened the bag and pulled out five pipes, some baking soda and a selection of burnt spoons. And some rocks. It was crack.

As my brother's friend put some water and some baking soda in the spoon I was disgusted but fascinated at their weird behaviour.

"I want to try it," I said.

"No fucking way," my brother said.

I got angry, and finally my persistence paid off. They loaded a pipe for me, and passed it over.

As I grabbed the pipe I looked up at them and said, "You fucking tell anyone, I'll shoot you!" I held the pipe to my lips as they coached me as to how to smoke it properly.

I couldn't get it right, so I threw the pipe against the wall, and flipped over the coffee table, knocking all the crack, cocaine, booze, and paraphernalia onto the floor. I threw a punch at my brother, and went to my room. "I can't even smoke crack right," I thought as I readied the biggest, fattest line of coke I'd ever done. My whole face went numb and I felt better and went back to the living room. I took a big shot of my whiskey and coke. "Okay, load me up," I said.

They asked if I was sure and I said yes. Putting the pipe to my lips I took a pull and held it in as long as I could. I let out the smoke slowly and waited.

Bam! My vision went blurry and my ears started to ring. Everything around me was muffled, and my heart raced. Euphoria! I had never felt that good in my life.

When I woke the next day, I was full of shame and guilt. Oh my God! I'm such a loser! I had just done something I said I would never do. I called them all and told them not to say a word, and to pretend it never happened.

I made a bit of money on the grow op, but the yield wasn't what was expected because I didn't have a clue what I was doing. The three months of paranoia were over.

Unfortunately, I was thinking about crack constantly. I wanted it, and I knew if Ken or Shannon found out I'd smoked it, it would be over for me. I'd lose everything.

CHAPTER 30

Life was going pretty good for me. I avoided all of Shannon's calls. I partied at the bar, and screwed random women. I played some sponge hockey in beer leagues, all the while drinking and doing coke. And I started smoking crack regularly.

The few of us that smoked crack kept it as a closely guarded secret from our other gang buddies. At the time, I didn't see why everyone couldn't just mind their own business. "I'll do whatever I want, leave me the fuck alone."

I knew Ken wasn't impressed with how I was behaving. He'd already sat me down when I had the grow op. He didn't know I was doing crack, but he knew my brother was hanging around my house. Ken didn't like my brother. My brother was hanging with a rival gang, and people in our circle thought he was a greasy crackhead. I shouldn't be allowing him into my house. If he was around me too much, people would think I was a greasy crackhead too.

CHAPTER 31

One day, my brother called and asked me to come down to a bar because he was there with my mom and dad. I said no and told him to fuck off. There was no way I was going to sit in a bar with them. The times I'd seen my parents at the bars around the neighbourhood, I'd hated it.

A while later, the bartender called, and told me to get down there. A guy was starting trouble with my mom, and my dad was in the middle of a fight.

I paged all of my bros, and loaded up my van with shotguns and baseball bats. As I got to the bar, two other vans pulled up and we all screeched to a stop, parked sideways in the parking lot and on the boulevard.

My chest was puffed out with relief at the loyalty and solidarity of my bros. We stormed the small pub, bursting through the doors together. I had a sawed off-pool cue, and was out for blood. Outnumbered and scared, the guy fighting my dad started backing off as my bigger buddy Kevin pushed him. Chaos ensued with people fighting and the asshole fighting my dad got punched to the ground. He got on top of my dad. When I saw that, I started clubbing him on the back of the head and kicking him in the face. I grabbed him by the hair while kicking him and giving him uppercuts. He got off my dad and ran behind the bar to call the police. The cops were on the way, and since my buddies were all on court conditions, they left.

Six police cars showed up and stormed the bar. They yelled at everyone to sit down. Nobody said a word, including the guy who started the whole thing. With blood on my face and legs the police pulled me outside and started questioning me trying to get me to say who my friends were.

"I got nothing to say. I have no idea who those guys were."

The cops told me if I didn't tell them, they would charge me.

"If you're going to charge me, do it. I wanna call my lawyer." I went back inside to my parents and brother.

My parents invited the troublemaker over to their table. He said sorry and shook my brother's and dad's hands, and gave my mom a hug. He bought a round of drinks, and leaned over to shake my hand. I batted it away and said, "Fuck you, you goof," and got up to leave.

Dad told me to sit the fuck down. I sat there and stewed. My family was clinking glasses with this guy? "Fuck this," I thought as I stood up. I pushed my brother, told him what a fucking bitch loser he was, and stormed out.

I met up with my buddies, and we talked about the fight as we drank and did coke into the night. We never talked about it again.

THE WEIGH-IN

CHAPTER 32

I really wanted a shirt that showed I supported the crew. I wanted to officially be recognized as a part of it. My head knew how dangerous the life was, but my friends in the biker gangs were as solid as you could come by.

One day, Ken called and told me to meet him out back of my house. I went out and jumped into his vehicle. He threw me a shirt and said, "Quit partying so much and smarten the fuck up. Don't fucking embarrass yourself." He told me he had shit to do, and I climbed out of his car.

I had made it! I knew the shirt was from his own collection. It was from one of the East Coast chapters, and this was a big deal. I was in!

I put the shirt on and sat in front of the mirror looking at myself for five minutes. I called my buddies and met them at a bar. I was proud, and wanted to show off. I felt like a superhero. I was invincible. I was going to control my drinking and fighting.

But with less booze in my system, I upped my cocaine use.

CHAPTER 33

We were sitting in a lounge one night when Ken leaned into me and said, "Roland, no fucking trouble tonight." I humbly agreed, as I respected him more than anything or anyone.

I was sitting with my back to the wall, surveying the crowd, when I noticed one of my brother's friends, Pete, on the other side of the bar. I hadn't seen him in years.

He'd clearly noticed me too, because he began walking towards our table. "Here we go," I thought, as he approached.

He grabbed me by the head and licked my face from chin to temple. I could feel my face flush as anger bubbled inside me. I stayed calm out of respect for my buddies. I looked at Ken, and he nodded. It was all I needed.

I jumped out of my chair and punched Pete so hard it knocked him down. I started kicking him in the head and in the stomach. As I lifted a chair over my head to slam down on him, I heard, "Roland! Put that fucking chair down and let's go. The cops are on the way!" I slowly put the chair down, grabbed Pete by the hair, and put my face in his.

"You see, you fucking bitch? You see what happens? I'm not a little kid anymore! All you goofs who beat me, teased me and harassed me, I'm coming for all of you one by one. You tell all of them they better watch out because I'm going to get all of you fuckers! I'm coming for them when they least expect it."

As we drove off, we saw police car after police car driving towards the bar. I pulled out some cocaine and cut it up on my cigarette pack. Bam! I snorted the line and yelled, "Fucking goof! Lucky I didn't shoot him."

CHAPTER 34

I felt insane half the time and was so very angry. I could keep up a good front while doing flooring jobs, and probably even came across as polite to the customers. A lot of the time though, I'd make up an excuse to finish early so I could go meet my buddy Brad at one of the bars. My attempts at not drinking and fighting were failing. One drink was enough to get everything cycling again.

I was with my buddies drinking when my pager went off: "911" and a phone number. I called it back and was told my brother and his pals were at a bar a few minutes away. I hopped in my van, snorted a line, and raced over to the bar.

I walked through the long line-up. A bouncer grabbed my arm and pointed to the pool tables, where my brother and his friends had gathered.

When I was in a rage, I would smell pepper. That smell made me angrier as I walked over to them.

I grabbed a pool cue with one hand and a ball with the other. I threw the ball at them, and broke the cue over my knee, holding the fat end as a weapon.

"What, what you guys got now, you fucking goofs? Why you running? You know what you did, fucking goofs!"

My friend Dave, who had seen me come in, came up beside me and said, "Roland, let it go. It's not worth it." We argued back and forth and then he hugged me. He wouldn't let me go, and I started crying.

He took me back to his table and put a drink in front of me. I downed it, and he convinced me to leave with him. As we were walking out to my van, he told me to cover my face with his jacket in an attempt to save me from embarrassment.

"You'll get them, Roland, just not now." He pulled out a bunch of cocaine and we did a big fat line. Satisfied with the night, I left and went home.

SUCKER PUNCHED

CHAPTER 35

Shannon started dating Mitch, who was a guy we went to school with. When I found out, I would call Shannon over and over obsessively. I hated the fact she was moving on. When they got engaged, my heart broke. Alcohol was the little devil on my shoulder, and one night it convinced me that driving to Shannon's apartment to confront them was a good idea.

I banged at the door until Mitch answered. I tried to push my way in, but Mitch stopped me. We started fighting in the hallway and he got the best of me. I remember looking up and seeing Shannon and Jesse looking at me. I felt so stupid and embarrassed. Shannon had found a real man, and he'd won. He'd won everything.

I jumped in my van and went back home. My roommate Jason was there and I asked him to back me up. As I loaded shotguns into the van, he tried to reason with me. He climbed in the van with me and continued talking. As I was heading back to Shannon's, I was overcome with guilt and embarrassment. When we pulled into the parking lot, I broke down. Jason consoled me, and with his help, I made the right decision to drive away.

When we got back to the house, my brain exploded. I trashed my room, while Jason went to his room downstairs. I grabbed a spoon and cooked up some crack. As I exhaled, I lay back in my bed. Finally. Peace.

As the high wore off, I was ravaged with guilt. I called Shannon over and over, but she would hang up.

I just wanted her to tell me everything was okay and that she wasn't mad at me.

CHAPTER 36

The upscale bars in Winnipeg's downtown soon became a staple for my growing drug sales. I was making a name for myself, and I was finally getting respect from everyone. As the saying goes, outward appearances do not necessarily reflect inward reality.

Inside, I was dying. I couldn't sleep at night, as I was afraid. People were coming to get me. People were after me. As I did when I was a kid, I'd barricade my bedroom door, or set up bottles in front of it so I'd hear if someone broke in.

When I did manage to sleep, I'd often wake up in tears from the nightmares of being raped. I don't know if it was physical or mental, but excruciating pain would seer through my rectum when I lay down. I would need to get out of bed and hunch over to make the pain go away.

My anger towards those who abused me grew. "I'm going to get those fuckers if it's the last thing I do," I would think to myself. I didn't feel I could talk to anyone about what happened. I had once told my uncle a little bit about what happened, but I never followed through, or sought any help.

FLASH KNOCKDOWN

CHAPTER 37

One hazy, hungover morning, my mother called and told me I had to get to the hospital. My dad had been in an accident at work.

I cleaned myself up, called Shannon and went to the Health Sciences Centre. My father was being transported from Portage la Prairie. I beat the ambulance and everyone else there.

When his ambulance pulled up, I ran to my dad. He was coherent, and was bitching about Walter, a co-worker who had apparently run him over. My dad was irritated and I knew to stay quiet. The paramedics told me to get out of the way. I was told to go to the waiting room and that I'd be told when my father was stabilized.

I called Shannon again, and she said she would be there soon.

Finally, I was allowed to see my dad. As I walked into his room, my tears started to flow.

"I'm okay, Roland. Stop crying!" he admonished.

I gave Dad a hug and pulled myself together. He was talkative, more than he'd ever been before. He told me how he was run over, and continued to bitch about Walter. But I could tell he was in a lot of pain. I'd never seen him like that before. He never talked that much, and I knew something was up.

He grabbed my hand, and increased the grip as he talked more and more to me. The skin on his palm was rough. He was so strong and his hard-working hands were full of earned calluses. It made me really uncomfortable, but I felt so loved by him at that moment. He asked about my mom and my brother. I could tell he was trying to console me from his hospital bed.

And then his eyes rolled back. His body seized and started shaking uncontrollable. I ran to the hallway and yelled for help.

Nurses and doctors came running into the room and told me to get out.

Mom, my brother, my Uncle Dan, and other family members started arriving at the hospital. Shannon arrived and she was a sight for sore eyes. She hugged me tight and took me outside. Just having her there made me feel better.

After a few cigarettes, we went back inside. The doctors asked if he had a drinking problem. My mother told them that he occasionally had some drinks. I interrupted and told the doctors he was an everyday drinker, for many years, drinking at least 12 beers and smoking two packs of cigarettes a day. They rushed back in the room and closed the door. We waited for what seemed like forever.

After a while Shannon went home. She still had a key to our house and I asked her to bring me back some essentials. We all went to see my dad. He was in a coma, and was on life support, with tubes going everywhere.

I knew I couldn't leave my dad. The nurses brought me a pillow and blanket. When everyone else had left and gone home, I kept trying to wake him up. "Jesse needs his grandpa…you can't die and leave us…wake the fuck up, you asshole!" I tried everything to get through to him, but nothing worked.

I was at the hospital for a week. I held his hand and told him not to be afraid.

A couple of buddies convinced me to take a break, and we went to the bar next door, having a few drinks and doing a few lines of cocaine. My pager went off, and I was called back to the hospital. It was time for the family to *decide*. It was time, and we knew my father wouldn't have wanted to live this way.

We went to say our goodbyes, and I remember the workplace insurance company asking my mom to sign papers.

We surrounded my father, and out of respect for my grandmother, a priest was called in to give my father his last rites.

We all held hands and the machines were turned off. I don't know how much time passed, but it seemed like days, as we watched him slowly slip away. It was October 12, 1994, and as he lay dying, I promised myself I was going to make my family proud. If it killed me, I was going to be a success.

A straight line across a monitor told me my father was dead. My brother and I left the hospital and went to the bar so that we could properly toast our dad.

CHAPTER 38

The weeks that followed my dad's death are a blur. I hadn't talked to Shannon in weeks. I hadn't seen Jesse in weeks. I promised to get him and didn't bother to show up. Shannon tells me he sat in his Jets hat, looking out the window, waiting for me.

I drank and filled my body with cocaine. My pager was going off incessantly, but I only got back to people I knew were up for partying. I didn't want to face reality.

But, I had to, to some extent. I had bills to pay. I got back to selling cocaine in the downtown bars.

Shannon called and said she wanted to talk to me. She wouldn't come to my house—our old house—so I cleaned myself up and met her at her mom's place.

"Rolly, I have something to tell you," she said. My mind raced in a thousand different directions.

I looked at her. "Okay. What the fuck? Tell me what's up!"

She told me she married Mitch over the weekend. My heart sunk and I felt like throwing up. She said she loved him, and that he was a good father to Jesse. My stomach churned.

"Mitch has been transferred, and we're moving to Thompson," she continued. "I love you, and I always will. I'll never keep Jesse from you, and you can visit any time you want."

She wanted me to be happy for her, and asked if I was okay.

I could feel the tears welling up in my eyes. "I can't believe you did this to me, Shannon. I need to go."

I drove two streets over, and parked my van as I couldn't see anything through the tears. I fell asleep in the van, and woke a few hours later.

I went home, poured a whiskey shot, and drank it down. Down to my stomach, and right up to my head. I snorted a fat line of cocaine, and felt the pain leave me. And then it dawned on me, no Shannon or no Jesse. I was free. I could do what I wanted, when I wanted, and my next conquest was to be recognized as a powerhouse gang member in Winnipeg! Fuck the World! So up my nose went another line of cocaine, and out I went to meet up with my bros. I told them the news, and the drinks were on them as we celebrated my freedom.

THROWING
HAYMAKERS

CHAPTER 39

I called in sick to the flooring company an awful lot. I could work my own hours to some extent, but my buddy Marcel had given me a lot of chances, and was getting to his breaking point. I was unaccountable and unreliable. But my cocaine sales were going well.

I pulled back from my mom once I started hearing stories of her frequenting the bars with my brother. He was doing massive amounts of cocaine, and I knew she was footing his debts. She'd finally received a settlement for my father's death. She'd been manipulated by the insurance company when my father was on his deathbed, so her settlement wasn't as large as it could be.

My brother was back in my mom's basement, taking advantage of her. When I'd drop into the local bars, I'd find them partying together. I hated it. I tried my best to mind my own business, but I knew it wasn't going to end well.

Sure, I did coke like my brother, but at least I wasn't a loser like him. Anger flowed through me.

Infuriated, I confronted them both on a regular basis, seeking them out at the bars in the neighbourhood. There was really not a whole lot I could do. I was again embarrassed by and for my family.

CHAPTER 40

I spent more time in the downtown nightclubs. At one of the clubs, I reconnected with my old friend Dino, who I knew well from my hockey days. The people I met in these clubs lived large. They were guys who liked to drink premium liquor, and weren't into any hard drugs. In these clubs, and with these guys, fights didn't break out. It was a new world to me.

I stayed close to my gang buddies too.

I was moving up in the drug-dealing world. I now had people working under me. I was living two lives.

CHAPTER 41

In 1996, some buddies from the downtown bar scene told Dino and me about a hair salon that wasn't doing very well. I was still angry my mother had spent so much money on my brother, and I wanted my piece of the pie too. But I wasn't going to take advantage of her that way. Instead, I decided to buy the salon. I didn't know a thing about the salon business, but I made all of the contacts, put a business plan together, and convinced my mother to co-sign a $60,000 loan.

Dino would run the salon, and I would keep doing flooring and selling cocaine for extra money. My plans for world domination were on! Look out, Winnipeg!

We looked at the location and it was beautiful. The setup was all in place. Chairs, mirrors, color stations, and some stylists were going to stick around if I took over. Nobody knew about my secret life as a drug dealer.

I knew nothing about hair, tanning, business, or how anything in the real world worked. Armed with hope and a dream, Runway 232 was born! I was going to be something if it killed me. I was going to have the best hair and tanning salon in Winnipeg.

I kept my drug and gang life separate from the salon (aside from stashing coke under the tanning beds), but juggling the two lives was exhausting. I had guys selling cocaine for me, and a salon full of staff to take care of. I was at the salon one day when I got the news a good friend from "my other life" was killed in a triple murder. I drank a lot with him and his friends, and it was pure luck I wasn't at his house when it happened.

The salon was starting to take off, but the first six months were tough. Dino ran the shop most of the time, and I would pop my head in just before closing to take care of the end of day.

I just wanted the salon to be successful to the point I could leave flooring and stop selling cocaine altogether. It didn't help things that Dino and I were both partyers. No matter where I was, I was surrounded by alcohol. I drank when I played sponge hockey, I drank with the salon staff, I drank with my gang buddies, and I drank with my other friends.

When the salon closed each night, we'd head across the street to drink at Earls. When we were finished at Earls, I'd sneak back to the salon to access my supply of coke.

Stocked up for the night, I would change out of my "nice" salon clothes into my supporter shirt and make my way to the bars, running a circuit between the downtown bars and the places my biker friends hung out. No matter where I was at the end of the night, I would find the after-party, be it at a biker booze can, or at a party condo above a high-end furniture store downtown.

Most of the time people kept away from me at the after-parties downtown. That was fine with me. I kept my temper under wraps when I was partying with the downtown clubbers, I wasn't looking for any trouble.

But at a party one night, this guy named Rob got under my skin. I could hear him harassing the women in the room, and my temper flared. Here this guy was treating everyone like shit, and nobody was doing a damn thing. "I'll fucking show people what solid means," I thought. Grabbing my beer bottle in one hand, I sized him up. He was a bigger guy, but that didn't scare me.

"Buddy, you better keep walking," I said as he walked past me. "For that matter, why don't you leave?"

He looked at me and laughed with his buddies. I looked at one of my friends, then turned to Rob and punched him. When he fell to the ground, I kicked him repeatedly. We were in a third-floor loft, and I grabbed him by the hair and dragged him to the open balcony door. People were screaming. As I got him closer to the balcony, I heard, "Roland, stop!" It was one of my downtown bar buddies. I punched the guy again, and left the party.

ON THE ROPES

CHAPTER 42

Thanks to the great work being done by the stylists Lori, Sherry, Mandy, Kevin, and my Aunt Michelle, the salon had grown. The chairs were always full, and the salon had won a few awards. Businesspeople, and even cops, flocked to our salon and bought tanning memberships. I chuckled to myself each time a cop came in to tan. He had no idea he was lying on top of thousands of dollars of coke.

I was invincible. I wasn't going to get caught, right?

To the outside world, it appeared I was running the most successful salon in Winnipeg, but by 1998, the salon's days were numbered. I was up to my eyebrows in debt, and I had to shut the doors. Between booze, cocaine and everything else I was pumping into my body, or in debt over, I couldn't make it work. It killed me to have to tell the staff that the salon was done.

When the salon doors closed that final day, my only source of income was the cocaine sales. I was really in trouble. Most of the profits I made from anything went right up my nose.

Every penny that didn't fly up my nose was already aimed at paying back the drug debts, and even with income from the salon, I could barely hold my head above water. The people selling drugs for me were bringing in more money than I was. Friends tried to talk to me about my cocaine use. I didn't listen. I was fucked.

CHAPTER 43

I had met her in 1997. At the downtown bars I frequented, there was a woman I always saw around. She was the most beautiful woman I ever laid eyes on. She was part of the *Ms. Eugena Swimwear Competition*, which was a local beauty pageant that toured around Winnipeg's hottest clubs. I followed her around like a puppy dog. Her name was Pamela, and I was determined to be with her.

She had an ex-boyfriend, and the tension was always high between him and me. Late one night, we ended up in a fight outside the bar. Surrounded by a crowd, we threw a few punches. Just like in the old days, pack mentality kicked in, and other brawls broke out around us. The fights broke up, and I drove home, drunk. I was in a sports car that I'd raced a few times at the Gimli Speedway, and it was hard to handle at the best of times, but even more when the person behind the wheel was drunk. I floored it as I hit the freeway. I let go of the clutch, and stepped on the gas. My car shot like a rocket and I lost control. The car launched fifteen feet in the air over the median and into oncoming traffic. It dropped like a bag of bricks popping one tire on each side. Cars swerved to miss me, and my car came to a stop. I got out to survey the damage. Other cars were stopped, and people ran up to me and asked if anyone was hurt. I told everyone I was okay, and asked for help in moving my car. One guy asked if I was drunk and I told him to mind his own business. We got my car to a side street, and I took off. I knew someone was going to call the cops.

Police came to my house shortly after I got home. I had turned off the lights and sat in the darkness waiting for them to leave. I had to be sober before I could talk to them.

As they were knocking, I did a line of cocaine which seemed to help my sore neck and back.

I downed half a bottle of cold medication so I could get to sleep. When I woke up, I concocted my story and called the police. I told them the car was too much to handle, and that I'd lost control and panicked. The police seemed to believe my story and I told them I would have my car towed from the side street. All clear. Now that I had the car situation taken care of, I started making calls to my buddies. I was going to get up on Pamela's ex. Arriving at a downtown bar that night, my biker friends with their colours, and me with my supporter shirt, stormed past the bouncers with no resistance.

I searched for him. He wasn't there, but another guy I had fought before was. I walked up to the guy, said a few words and popped him in the mouth. He dropped and we scattered out of the bar, because we knew police were on their way. As we drove off, five police cars pulled up.

I couldn't move my hand and I went to the hospital. I'd broken my hand when I punched him. I was fit with a cast and sent on my way.

CHAPTER 44

Pamela had no idea what my life was really like. She wasn't the type of woman who would want to be with me if she knew the truth. She was a good woman, and I wanted her more than anything. I fell in love immediately, and started cleaning up my act.

I trusted her. She'd met my son, and I felt safe with her. She knew nearly everything about me. *Nearly everything*. We were lying in bed when I told her I had been abused by a boxing coach. Silence. She didn't know what to say. I felt exposed and vulnerable.

When she left that day, I felt broken. I'd blown it. There's no way she could love me now. Thank God I didn't tell her about the other predators, about my brother, about being tied down and abused.

But she didn't leave me. Instead, I did my very best to push her away. I had made myself too vulnerable. I'd told her too much. I'd go through a cycle of pushing her away, and then become overly needy. It had to be confusing for her, and eventually, we stopped talking.

She was gone and so was my hope.

"Way to go, Roland, you screwed up another thing. You're such a loser. You can't do anything right."

My debts were piling up. I had some sporadic flooring jobs, but my cocaine use and drinking were increasing. I wasn't paying my mortgage or any bills. I couldn't go to my mom, because she was broke after bailing out my brother and helping me with the salon. I was finished.

And then I was served. My house was being seized if I didn't come up with the back payments.

Not long after, my house went dark. I owed too much to the utility company.

I called some friends and gathered some candles. I sat in the dark, licking my wounds and doing drugs with my buddies into the wee hours of the morning. When my friends left, I did more drugs and loaded my rifle. I cried as I wrote Jesse a note, letting him know how much I loved him and his mother. I told him I was sorry for being so weak. I downed mouthfuls of cough syrup which made me groggy.

I put the loaded gun in my mouth and attempted to maneuver it so I could pull the trigger with my toe. I didn't have enough strength to accomplish the task, and fell back into my bed, with the hopes of never waking up again.

I have no idea how many hours (or days) I slept, but when I woke up, it was dusk. I got dressed and went to make some calls from a nearby phone booth. When I got back to my house, I unhooked the oven. "You can take my house but you can't take my oven, you pricks!"

I loaded what I could into my van: the oven, my hunting equipment, some clothes, some blankets, and some memorabilia. I was 28 years old, and I was completely broke and completely broken. I couldn't work in flooring anymore because my hockey injuries and addiction haunted me. My mind was more broken than my body, and the only thing that helped me was being numb from cocaine or alcohol.

"Way to take over the world, Roland," I thought, as I drove away. Within a day, I was living in my van on the side streets near my house.

PLAYING POSSUM

CHAPTER 45

I was still clinging to my dreams of being a full patch biker. I frequented club houses and was being groomed to step up to the plate and do something with my connections. The biker wars were in full force in Manitoba and I was right in the middle of the action. My chance to get that patch was being handed to me.

By this time I had reconnected with my childhood friend Colin. He was selling drugs too, and I knew he'd had some experience with crack and cocaine. I knew his family well, as I played hockey with his older brother Corwin, and had even gone to his house during lunch hours in elementary school.

I'd asked Colin if I could stay with him. He was hesitant, but felt obligated to help me. We would spend days on end smoking crack. Both of us were trying to make a go selling drugs, but our own addictions were taking over. Colin had to sell his house to pay his drug debts. He moved in with his girlfriend, and I moved in with our friend Sean.

That's when the shit really hit the fan. Sean, Colin, and I smoked a quarter pound of crack, and I was up for days. And then Sean introduced me to Tracy, a crackhead prostitute.

CHAPTER 46

When 2000 rolled around, I was hitting bottom. I couldn't stop using cocaine. I couldn't stop drinking. My drug debts were piling higher.

It was getting so bad, friends were holding pieces of crack for me so that I wouldn't smoke away my profits.

I needed my high. I needed cash, so I did anything I could to make money, and I took over collecting a drug debt for Colin. It was supposed to be easy. I recruited a couple of my up-and-coming biker buddies to come with me. The guys we met in the back lane weren't quite willing to pay up. They started beaking off, so we pulled out our clubs and bats. They ran. I gave chase, and caught up to one of them. He turned and swung at me with a knife. I swung my bat and dropped under his strike. As I got back up he swung the knife again. It was going towards my midsection as I raised my leg. Then he ran off.

When I got back to Sean's place, I felt a warm liquid on my leg, and my shoe felt wet. I lifted my pants, and my friends took a look at my leg. The gash was so deep you could see muscle in the wound.

I drank a few shots of whiskey and headed to the hospital.

I sat in the waiting room for hours. The police came and asked what had happened. I told them I had tripped.

My leg was frozen, I was stitched up, and sent home.

It wasn't over. The hunt was on for the guy who slashed me. My buddies and I spent a few nights searching the city. No success.

CHAPTER 47

I needed to make money or I was going to be in big trouble. I figured out the perfect way.

I had a couple of buddies take me to a bar. I told them to wait for me in the back lane. I jumped out of the vehicle with my shotgun, stormed the doors, and headed to the gambling machines. I told everyone to get on the floor. Everyone dropped and the clerk emptied all the registers into the bag I was holding. I bolted as fast as I could into the night, down the back lane to my waiting ride.

We screamed with excitement at the score. What a rush! I had never felt a rush like that ever. Fighting didn't even come close to giving me that feeling.

We met up with some dealers and started a three-day bender. When everyone was gone, and I was coming down, I felt nothing but guilt. I never wanted to be that way and the crime I committed was nothing short of disgusting. What if Shannon found out? What if my mom found out?

I searched Sean's house for drugs or booze. I found a bottle of Tylenol. I emptied the bottle into my hand and washed the pills down with warm, half-drunk beer, hoping I'd taken enough to kill me.

I woke up, not knowing where I was. I stumbled out into the winter night in my socks and made way to my neighbour's door. My friend Kevin answered, and I pushed my way in and collapsed on his couch. The next thing I remember is paramedics asking me what I took, and flashing a light in my eyes. I told them I took pills, and they whisked me off in an ambulance.

Waking up in the hospital room I had no idea where I was or what exactly happened. A nurse came over and I asked why I had a needle in my arm. She said I was dehydrated, told me to not worry, and to go back to sleep.

I was on suicide watch. I put my arm over my face so people couldn't look at me. My mouth was so dry and every part of my body hurt.

Days ran into one another, and I have no idea how long I was in the hospital. Memories of the past week, and memories of abuse ran through my mind on a loop. My Uncle Dan came to visit. We talked a bit, and again I told him that I'd been abused when I was younger. Unless I was willing to get help for my addictions and everything else, there was little he could do.

After he left, I made my way to the phone and called some of my bros. I didn't tell them what had happened, or why I was in the hospital, just that I was there. I called Colin and told him that I needed something bad, but that I couldn't leave the hospital. Within an hour, the nurse told me I had a visitor. Colin came in and slipped me a makeshift pipe and some crack. I hid it away until the night.

When I was sure I was in the clear, I got out of bed and pretended I was going to the bathroom. I made my way to the stairwell, climbed the stairs to the highest floor, and set up shop to get high. I lit the lighter and took the biggest hit of my life. My head rang and I fell down on my ass as paranoia set in. I tried a few more times but couldn't get the high I needed.

Jumping out of my skin, I went back to bed. I needed to get out of the hospital. I got my stuff all together, made a call, and a friend picked me up outside the hospital.

```
Sask. Information and Library Services C
                RECEIPT
        Patron: Ferchuk, Cory
            05-30-2015 1:36PM

INVOICE #: 520537
STATUS: Overdue
DESCRIPTION: Indian Ernie : perspectives
AMOUNT OWED: $4.20
AMOUNT PAID: $4.20
BALANCE: $0.00


Total Paid: $4.20
```

Kent Brown and Roland coaching Team Manitoba Boxing
for the 2011 Canada Winter Games in Halifax

Roland coaching Team Manitoba, Halifax 2011 Canada Winter Games

Roland and Uncle Dan Vandal

Roland out for a cruise on his Harley Davidson fat bob

Roland speaking at an Anti Bullying event.
Picture by HOW (Humans of Winnipeg)

Roland Vandal and childhood hockey coach
Al Claydon 30 years later

Roland with Shannon and Jenna

Tracey and Leslie, my youth home professional supports

HOW photoshoot with Jesse and Roland

(from left) Karen, Roland, Kristin and Wayne

30 plus year friends Monty Taylor, Chris Davis Sean Wright,
hockey coach Al Clayton

COVERING UP

CHAPTER 48

I had found out about a grow operation that was ready to be harvested. I'd met some people at raves and parties, and I knew they were ballsy enough to raid it with me.

We knew the grow op was being watched, but people partied there all the time. Late one night six of us sat in my van and scoped it out. When the time was right, we loaded our shotguns and rifles and ran up the alley. We all hid around the side of the house and one person knocked on the door. My heart was racing. The door opened and we rushed into the house yelling for everyone to get on the floor. There were pitbulls in the house, and we told them to put the dogs away.

I hovered over the five people on the floor, waving my gun, and thought to myself, "What the fuck am I doing? What have I become?"

Soon my buddies came running upstairs with pails full of pot. "If any of you say anything or follow us, you're going to get shot," my buddy said.

We ran down the back lane to our car and sped off. None of us spoke about it again. It was the code of the street, and the code was all we had.

CHAPTER 49

Things didn't get better after we raided the grow op. Colin and I were both in deep and he owed a lot of money.

One day, as we were hanging out, the door was kicked in. They were there for Colin, and he was quickly put to the ground. A screwdriver came out and I was certain we were both goners. Colin was told he had used up all his chances, and if he didn't pay up, the next time he saw these guys it would be different.

I knew I was next.

CHAPTER 50

I was a broke, homeless crackhead with nothing. I partied a lot with Tracy because she had ways to get us high for free. Sean, Colin and I spent days on end at her house on the north side of Winnipeg. I couldn't stay with Sean anymore, so I effectively moved into her house. Some rich guy would hang around, spending thousands of dollars on drugs, and we took full advantage.

Soon she was evicted, and I lost my free place to stay. I made a few calls and I was able to stay with my Uncle Denis and Aunt Jeanette. They did their best to nurse me back to health, but I was so uncomfortable, I left after a few nights. I remember how hurt Uncle Denis looked as I drove away.

I got ahold of Tracy, and found out she was at a hotel. She was partying with the rich guy. I had nothing to offer. I wanted to drink and get high, so I made my way to the hotel.

The room smelled awful. People were passed out and I remember feeling lonely. I got a few smiles, but I don't think anyone was happy to see me. I doubt they had even noticed I was gone. I grabbed a bottle and took a big chug. It warmed my stomach and hit my head like a ton of bricks.

I told everyone not to talk to me. I sat there with a knife in hand, smoking crack and waiting for something to happen. I didn't trust Tracy, and was certain she was setting us up. I *knew* the people I was with would have killed me if they'd gotten the chance.

We switched hotels when we felt things were getting too heated. We were dealing drugs, and buying drugs, and we couldn't get caught. Tracy would make a call, and a cab driver would deliver crack to her. I would deliver crack to people who called us.

I found myself going down to meet some dealers at the back of the hotel. Something didn't feel right, and I was on guard, ready for the worst. I had my hunting axe in my jacket, just in case.

I asked them if they had the drugs, and they told me no. They said I should give them the money, and they'd be right back with the crack.

"What, do you think I'm stupid?" I asked.

The smell of pepper filled my nose, and I pulled out my axe. One of them pulled out a knife, and it was on. I backed myself against the building and started swinging. I could tell the guy who'd pulled out the knife wasn't prepared to use it. They ran off, and I followed, swinging the axe the whole time. It glanced off one of their arms as they rounded a corner and darted into a cab.

I went back to the room and told everyone we had to leave.

LOW BLOWS

CHAPTER 51

We spent the next while with Tracy. We spent our time getting high in hotel rooms, or travelling in cabs, delivering crack. I was always armed and ready for the worst.

During a delivery, we stopped to get booze, and I guess it looked like we were up to no good. Colin and Sean went into the liquor store, and apparently the clerk thought they were there to rob it. Sean and Colin came running out, and we were long gone before the cops showed up.

We had the cab drop us at a nearby crackhouse. I remember the scene and atmosphere. Everyone was stoned out of their minds, on coke and on ecstasy. Techno music blared, and people were dancing all over like wild animals. I drank as much alcohol as I could and sat with my back to the wall, ready, just in case anything went down.

I took some X too.

CHAPTER 52

May 8, 2002

My bigtime dreams of being a full-patched biker were over. I was frequenting booze cans and crackhouses looking for a high. I was hanging with street gangs and drug runners, and was completely separated from the biker life. They'd tried. I'd been sat down many times and told that my drinking and cocaine use was out of control. I was damned if I didn't stop, but I couldn't. I wasn't going to stop. Thoughts of repairing my life became too much to fathom.

I threw myself into violent situations, hoping I would die. By this time I'd got my hands on a handgun, and I would sit in the hotel rooms we partied in hoping for an opportunity to kill someone, better yet, hoping someone would kill me. I'd leave only to do an armed robbery, nothing big, just big enough to feed my habit.

Sitting in a downtown hotel one night, Tracy placed an order for crack cocaine through a phone line some of my old buddies ran. She told the dealer I was with her.

Next thing I knew a loud knock came on the hotel room door. I thought to myself, "This is it," and put the handgun under a pillow as Tracy opened the door. It was my friend Marvin and another guy. Marvin looked at me and said, "Roland, are you okay? It's over, Roland. Let's go. I'm getting you out of here."

I told him I wasn't leaving, and that he should go and leave me alone.

Marvin shook his head and gave me a big hug. Tears fell from my eyes, and I told him to leave and to leave me alone. He nodded, and told me I had to stop. I knew he was right, but I was embarrassed. I used to be something, and now all I was was a loser crackhead who couldn't even afford to use a payphone.

A few days later, Tracy, Sean and I went to deliver crack to a hotel in the low-track area of town. While I was walking into the hotel, my dad's favourite song, "Cat's in the Cradle," was playing over and over in my head. I thought it was a sign, and thought to myself that I was probably going to die that day.

We walked up the stairs and banged on the door. A voice asked, "Who is it?" Tracy said her name and they let us in. The smell was overwhelming. The room was connected to two other hotel rooms with doors in between. I was wearing my supporter shirt, so that made me feel safe. That shirt was my armor.

The room was full of nicely dressed women and various types of men. The women were grabbing guys by the hands and pulling them into the bedrooms. Jesus Christ, what have we walked into? I had heard about shit like this, but never seen it before. A woman who seemed to be organizing everything came up to me and asked me if I wanted to be taken care of. She must be the madam, I thought.

I told her that I was okay and to leave me be. Tracy sensed how uncomfortable I was, so she took Sean and me to another room. The madam followed. We smoked some crack and the madam again asked if I was okay. I told her if the place was what I thought it was, I was going to have to leave.

The madam rubbed my back and told me to lie back in the bed.

"Listen, fuck, I'm not here for that," I said. "If anyone touches me I'm going to flip the fuck out!"

She backed off, and Sean told me to relax. I showed him the knife under my shirt and said, "If anyone comes near me from that other room I'm gonna do something, and you know I will!" The madam opened the door between the rooms and told everyone to stay out.

Crisis averted, we stayed there for three days, smoking crack and drinking whiskey. I took pills, none of which I recognized, and did ecstasy. My mind was full of suicidal thoughts. I didn't kill myself. I just got high.

WHAT THE FUCK IS THAT?

Eyes were watching me. There were demons everywhere.

I told myself to stop being paranoid, and convinced myself it was something I'd seen in a movie.

"I need some air," I said.

As I walked to the door, a guy asked me where the fuck I was going. I put my hand inside my shirt and pulled out my knife. "I have to get out of here," I said.

A voice behind me said to let me out but not to let me back in.

The elevator was taking too long, so I hurried to the stairs. Exiting into a back lane, the cold stung my skin and the sun burned my eyes.

I had no place to go. I wandered the streets, stopping and resting in bus shacks, pretending to wait for the bus. I didn't sleep, and I had no idea how long I'd been on my own.

Walking down a back alley, I pulled out my knife and put the blade to my chest. If only I had the courage to run into a wall. I prayed for the strength to do it, and for it to not look like a suicide. If I did it right, people would think I'd been killed while being robbed.

I heard voices approaching and put the knife away.

I kept walking, trying to figure out where to go. I needed to find Tracy again. By now she must have moved to another hotel.

I was thirsty, so I went into a restaurant and used the bathroom. I washed my face and drank water from the tap. I left the restaurant and made my way towards the river. I sat on the bank and tried to calm down and rest. It was cold, but I had to pull myself together. I kept thinking of Jesse, and how he was going to grow up without a father. I didn't want that, but I knew I had nothing to offer anyone.

I stopped at a store and asked to use the phone.

I called everyone I could, and finally got ahold of Sean. They were all still partying and I asked him to come and get me. He asked me where I was because I'd been gone for two days.

Sean came and picked me up. "What the fuck, Roland? Where have you been?" I told him I didn't want to talk about it and asked for a smoke. It was one of the best cigarettes I've ever had. Not much else was said, and we went to another hotel. Tracy was there with her rich friend.

I went to the bathroom and threw up. Looking at myself in the mirror, I didn't even recognize myself. I washed my face over and over, and grabbed a razor and shaved off the scruff. I hopped into the shower and let the hot water fall over me. It felt so good. I didn't want to leave the bathroom. I eventually found the courage.

Tracy gave me a hug and sat me down on the couch. She asked me if I wanted a hoot, and the other people in the room encouraged me to have one. A bottle of whiskey was handed to me, and I took a swig. I felt sick. Then it came. I started to throw up in my mouth. I ran to the bathroom, and hugged the toilet. I kept thinking of my mother, and what it would be like for her if I drowned in toilet water. I cleaned myself up and went back out to the room. A drink was put in front of me, and the pipe was passed over.

I don't remember a lot of what happened after that but when I woke up, only a few people were left in the room. Tracy's rich buddy was there, and I asked him where everyone was. He said they'd been gone a while. I told him we had to leave. We packed up some duffle bags and left.

We climbed into a cab that was out front of the hotel. I asked the rich guy if he had money for the cab. When he said yes, I told the cab driver to take us to the Norvilla.

BACK IN THE RING

CHAPTER 53

When I woke up in that hotel room, there was no chance I could return to any semblance of normal physical, mental, or emotional health.

I've been sober since May 15, 2002.

I'm astonished I survived. I'm astonished I was never charged with a crime as an adult. I wonder how I never killed anyone. I was an animal, full of alcohol, drugs, and rage.

But I did survive, remarkably. After a 10-day stay in hospital, Linda welcomed me back into her home. I stayed with her until a bed opened up at the Addictions Foundation Manitoba Treatment Centre, where I spent 28 days. Then I spent 60 days at Tamarack Recovery Centre. The staff and counsellors at both saved my life.

I've been sober since May 15, 2002.

I found out later I'd had a massive seizure, and I was very lucky to be alive. Calling my mom saved my life.

I've been sober since May 15, 2002.

Getting psychological help saved my life.

I've been sober since May 15, 2002.

Talking with professionals about the abuse I'd suffered and sharing my story with other victims saved my life.

I've been sober since May 15, 2002.

Freedom for me started with my last drink, and with that last hit off the pipe. Sobriety saved my life.

As I write this, I've almost convinced myself that I didn't really have an issue with alcohol. I'm powerless over alcohol, and climbing twelve huge steps saved my life.

I've been sober since May 15, 2002.

And, returning to boxing saved my life. After I left Tamarack, I was inspired and motivated, and was given a job working the front desk at Pan Am Boxing Club. The place where I'd met the man who first abused me became my second home.

Returning to the ring hurt. My hands, my ribs, my shoulders, and my head hurt constantly, but boxing was an amazing form of release. My days were dedicated to boxing and recovery.

I wasn't far into recovery when I realized that what I put into the world was important. If I am good, loving, caring and compassionate, that is exactly what the world will give back to me. I was renewed. I was reborn and began dedicating my life to giving back.

Over a decade sober, I'm still learning about the higher power. I have a fundamental idea of God, and have learned that if I put other people first—if I reach out, if I offer support—God will ensure that all my needs are met. If I love, I will be loved.

I've been sober since May 15, 2002.

CHAPTER 54

While I was at the Addictions Foundation of Manitoba, my body screamed. Every injury I'd ever had ached. The pain was constant, and I was sent for x-rays. The x-rays showed all my old injuries: multiple hand fractures, seven broken ribs, and a broken collar bone. My knees were a mess from hockey. While a lot of what I was feeling was related to those old injuries, the pain was also a manifestation of my mental anguish.

I was introduced to Tracey, who would be my counsellor. After a few sessions, she told me if I wasn't going to open up and participate, I would have to leave the program.

I got two words out and the floodgates opened. I cried for hours.

During one of our sessions, Tracey recommended I find myself a sponsor.

I'd seen a guy hovering around the smoking doors, and wondered, "Who's this fucking tree hugger?" Tracey introduced us. His name was Ian. With one week left at AFM, I asked him to be my sponsor.

He said yes.

I told Tracey that after AFM, I'd have nowhere to go. Tracey secured me a bed at Tamarack.

I was terrified to leave AFM, and placed the first of many calls to Ian. I asked him for a ride to Tamarack.

When he dropped me off, he told me to call him whenever I needed to.

CHAPTER 55

When I was in Tamarack, I was broke. I had three garbage bags full of my belongings, and nothing else. I hadn't filed a tax return in five years. My credit was terrible, and I owed Shannon $6,000 in child support. I had no idea how to fix things. I'd asked Shannon to call off the dogs at Maintenance Enforcement, but she refused. More tough love from Shannon, and it was just what I needed. I had to grow up and take responsibility. I had to provide for our son. I realized getting sober was the simple part, but repairing what I had damaged would take a long time.

I knew I had to get my finances in order to be able to provide for my son.

I went to the Revenue Canada office and spent two hours outside its doors, smoking and pacing the sidewalk. When I mustered the courage to go in, I asked to speak to someone who could help me straighten my life out. Verging on tears, I told the agent I was homeless. I told him I was an addict and alcoholic. He met my honesty with empathy and understanding. He told me the situation wasn't as bad as I thought.

He asked for my social insurance number. I told him I had no documents, and no records. I wouldn't be able to provide anything to show any income I'd had over the past five years. My anxiety was through the roof.

He told me I was doing the right thing and that he would help me. As he punched my social insurance number into the computer, I wanted to escape.

"Run, Roland. Get out of here," I thought as he got up from his desk and left the office. I forced myself to stay. Thoughts of how disappointed my father would be filled my head, and I knew I had to make things right.

The agent returned and handed me three envelopes. "Roland, your mountain is only a molehill," he said. He told me I owed about $16,000 and that arrangements could easily be made. I told him it would be hard for me to find that kind of money. He wrote something on a piece of paper and handed it to me.

"I really shouldn't be doing this," he said.

When I looked down, it was for an agency that would help me declare bankruptcy.

When I left his office, I felt as though a weight had been lifted from my shoulders. The sky was so blue. The air smelled so good. I held my head high and said "hello" to people on the street. I had finally been honest with someone.

When I returned to Tamarack, reality set in. Despite what the kind man at Revenue Canada told me, I was significantly in debt. I lay on my bed and cried. Thoughts of suicide ran through my brain. "Snap out of it, Roland," I told myself. I couldn't do that to Shannon. I couldn't do that to Jesse. I couldn't do that to my family. I couldn't be that selfish.

I got up and took a walk down by the river. Making sure no one saw me, I ducked behind a tree, fell to my knees and invited God into my life.

"Show me what to do and I'll do it!" I got up, brushed myself off, and walked back to the treatment home feeling down but feeling really good at the same time.

I called Ian.

THE RUBBER MATCH

CHAPTER 56

When Ian left, my mind felt clearer than it had ever been before. I sat down and made a list of everything I needed to do: Exercise. Fix finances. Declare bankruptcy. Get a job. Make amends. Help others.

Ken was at the Remand Centre, and I knew I had to see him. I owed him money, and I owed him respect, and I owed him an apology. He'd given me so many chances and had done all he could to help me get my act together. I'd fucked it all up.

I went and saw him at the jail. I apologized, and promised to pay him back.

"I'm glad you're okay, Roland," he said. "I'm proud of you."

I vowed to him that I would help others. "I want to help kids. I want to talk to schools."

He told me he was glad I got help, and that I should help as many people as I could.

I promised to pay back every cent I owed to him. As I got up to leave, he said, "Consider it over, you don't owe me anything, Rolly."

Heading back to Tamarack, I thanked God for the opportunity. I thanked God for surrounding me with stand-up people like the man to whom I'd just said goodbye.

CHAPTER 57

As soon as I left Tamarack, I declared bankruptcy and registered for social assistance. With a bus pass in my pocket, I was on my way to taking my life back.

It had been nearly 20 years since I stepped in the ring. I was completely out of shape the day I walked back through the doors of the Pan Am Boxing Club. I was going to change that. I was going to be competitive again.

I didn't have the money to renew my boxing career, so I asked Harry Black, the president of the club, if I could volunteer in lieu of payment. He agreed, and after a few months, Harry hired me to work part-time. I now had a little bit of money, and was on my way.

I wanted so badly to be a good person, but flashbacks and negativity would infiltrate my good thoughts over and over again. Peace seemed to only come at 12 step meetings and at the boxing club.

At the time I'd returned to the club, Donny Lalonde was making a comeback. Uncle Dan had introduced me to Donny when I was a kid, and I respected him a lot. I asked Harry to let me be involved in promoting Donny's fights. I was given the job of approaching businesses to sponsor blocks of tickets that would later be given to youth groups within the city. Donny dubbed it "The Roland Vandal Inspiration Initiative," and I truly was inspired. My commitment to serving others grew.

I wanted to do more, but without a car, my opportunities to serve others were limited. I prayed.

"God, if I can get a car, I promise to help people with it." Not long after, my prayer was answered. My dear friend Monty was selling his old car, and told me I could make payments directly to him, when I had the money.

I began driving people from AFM to 12 step meetings. I carried a shovel with me and would clear random driveways. It felt good. I felt better about myself.

I began picking up odd jobs here and there. I did some work for my sponsor Ian at the apartment blocks he owned. I did small jobs at the salon my friend Sherri owned.

After nearly one year sober, I decided it was time to get back to real work. I called a former flooring boss and told him I was in treatment.

"If I get to one-year sober, will you hire me back?"

Nearly to the day of my sobriety, I began work as a flooring installer. Around the same time, a woman who I had a one-night stand with two years before contacted me and let me know I had a son, Jaicey.

CHAPTER 58

Installing floors got me back on my feet financially, and I began to pay off my debts and make financial amends. I owed so many people—Chris, Monty, my mom, my aunt and uncle, my employees from the hair salon, and most importantly, Shannon and Jesse.

When I cleared my debts, I began sponsoring men in the 12 step movement. I began speaking at schools, telling my story of transformation.

I started boxing competitively again.

In the ring, I'd often have flashbacks. During one bout, my family came to cheer me on. I was winning when I noticed my brother out the corner of my eye. I instantly felt dirty, and memories flooded my brain. I gave up, walked to my corner, and had Harry remove my gloves.

I asked the higher power to guide me. I never wanted to give up again.

SAVED BY THE BELL

CHAPTER 59

I continued with boxing. I was 32 and would soon be competing in the World Ringside Championships in Kansas City. I was sober and motivated to win the tournament to prove to myself I had conquered all my demons.

When we arrived in Kansas City, we discovered my coach had mistakenly registered me in a lower weight class, and there was no way to change it. I would have to lose 11 pounds overnight to qualify.

I immediately began working out, skipping with my limbs covered in plastic. I soaked in the hot tub. I sat in the sauna. And I skipped some more. I refused water and food.

At weigh-in, we found out I qualified to fight in the lower weight class. I drank as much water as I could, and prayed for strength.

When my first bout began, I pushed the negative thoughts and memories as far down as I could and left the corner like a freight train. I won the first round and did well in the second. I was exhausted.

"Two more minutes, Roland," said Cory, my corner man. I gave it everything I had. The bell went, and I won with a unanimous decision. I went to the dressing room and when I got outside, I found a quiet spot, fell to my knees, and thanked God.

I was so happy, but was exhausted physically, mentally, and emotionally. I'd have to make weight again tomorrow, and the thought terrified me. I didn't want to let my coach and teammates down, but I knew I couldn't do it. I withdrew from the competition. I felt like a failure, and wanted a drink.

"No, Roland," I told myself. I was 15 months sober.

CHAPTER 60

I met Dr Jim Simm in 2003. Dr Simm is an addictions psychiatrist and he told me it was okay for me to express myself and to share my story. "We are only as sick as our secrets," my friend Lauren once said. It took a long time for me to heed their advice.

In November 2003, I fought in Edmonton at the Western Canadian Championships, and my past was still clearly an emotional liability. I made the finals and was winning the fight when, in the third round, I was hit with a flashback. I took a hit to the face, and faked its severity so that the ref would call the fight.

In April 2004, I fought at home. It was my sixth amateur fight, and my Uncle Dan and cousin Doug were in the stands. I fought hard and came out with the win.

I set my sights on the Ringside Native North America Tournament in Lawrence, Kansas in July. I trained my ass off, but my brain was looking for excuses not to compete. My coaches knew I was struggling mentally and worked to prepare me for the match. I was as physically ready as I could be and on weight. I was not going to let my past control me anymore.

The bell rang and it was on. With relentless, tactful pressure I dominated the bout. I thanked God when I was declared the winner of the tournament. When the referee raised my arm in victory, it felt as though an anvil had been taken off my shoulders.

CHAPTER 61

I was still having flashbacks, and was ravished with guilt, but I was able to function.

While in treatment, I'd dreamed of opening a recovery home, and I was bound and determined to do it.

Ian and I opened 210 Recovery in 2005. In 2008, I had some semblance of financial stability and was able to purchase a house and open my own men's home. I wanted to help kids with similar lives as me, so I soon switched focus and turned my men's home into a foster treatment home for high risk teens.

But I hadn't overcome my demons. I was still in denial.

TOE TO TOE

CHAPTER 62

I was well submerged in the 12 step movement and shared stories of my past traumas at each meeting. Outside of the meetings, I did my best to keep the negative thoughts at bay. When I was busy, the thoughts weren't there, so I immersed myself in work, volunteering, and boxing. I was taking counseling courses, and, having realized the best way to face my demons was to become a boxing coach myself, I started working towards my level 3 coaching certification. I realize now I kept busy because I was too afraid to sit down, alone, with myself.

I was still actively seeking approval, from my dead father and everyone else. I knew I was in trouble, and asked Manitoba Health to secure a spot for me at Homewood Health Centre, in Guelph, Ontario. Homewood was one of Canada's premier psychiatric hospitals, and I knew I could get the help I needed there. There was a waiting list. So, I waited.

I had dated a bit during the first five years of my recovery, but I was terrified of letting anyone get too close.

The relationships were brief, and I hurt a lot of good women. I hurt myself, too. I get attached easily and when my head and heart fought about pushing these women away, my head always won. It took me a long time to learn just because I was lonely, or looking to get laid, it didn't mean I needed to take advantage of someone's feelings. Women weren't pieces of meat. Women weren't toys I could play with.

In 2008, I met Kaley. We hit it off right away, and I fell in love. My heart beat my head in that fight.

We met at a 12 step fellowship, and it turned out her father had once dated my aunt. I met her whole family, and everything seemed perfect.

CHAPTER 63

Kaley had a son, Spencer, and the three of us were inseparable. I met and loved her mom Vernelle, and her dad, Jerome. Kaley and I moved in together, and I was over the moon.

Kaley wanted more children, and I didn't share with her that I wasn't interested in becoming a father again. I was working to rebuild my relationship with Jesse, and I couldn't imagine putting another child through what I'd put Jesse through. Despite realizing I should treat women with respect and honesty, I was completely blind to the fact I wasn't going to be able to fulfill her wants and needs. In reality, I wasn't back on my feet enough to support myself, let alone Kaley and her son.

When I'd see Jerome with Spencer, it reminded me of my father and Jesse, and part of me believed if I could get Kaley to marry me, I'd have a father again. I went to Jerome and asked if I could have his blessing to marry Kaley. He shook my hand, and welcomed me to the family. He owned a jewelry store, and we made plans for me to visit and pick out a ring.

I invited friends and family to a comedy club. I had met with the manager, and arranged for the comedian to work the proposal into his routine.

Kaley said yes.

Shortly after we became engaged, Manitoba Health notified me they had secured my spot at Homewood.

I was broken, leaving Kaley and Spencer behind, but knew I needed treatment. Lying in the hospital bed the first night, I thought of Kaley. I wondered what I was doing there. Why had I left her? I had no one but myself to blame for anything.

The next day, while outside having a smoke, I decided I had to leave. Here I was, surrounded by people who knew how sick I was, and I knew best. I missed Kaley so much.

I packed up my stuff and asked to see the doctor. I told him I felt like a lab rat and needed to leave. He asked if there was anything he could do to convince me to stay. I shook my head and told him I'd already booked my flight.

As I sat on the plane, a feeling of impending doom took over. I wasn't close to being better. I shouldn't have left. I had fucked up again. Kaley didn't deserve a broken man.

When I got back to Winnipeg, I had no real explanation for anyone. Our relationship grew strained, and we split up.

I moved back in with my Aunt Jeanette. I hadn't been back at Jeanette's place that long when Kaley called and told me her dad had passed away. We got back together for a spell, but our relationship never recovered. I blew it.

CHAPTER 64

Even within the recovery movement I couldn't find many who understood my thinking. A lot of the time, *I* didn't understand my thinking.

To everyone around me, it seemed as though I was getting my life back together, but on the inside, I was the loneliest person in the world. I was overwhelmed, and nothing was working.

I busied myself more, going to counselling at the Men's Resource Centre. I took addictions courses, coaching courses, and safety officer courses. Anything I could do to keep my mind on track. Anything I could do to overpower the negative thoughts.

At the Men's Resource Centre I learned 93% of people who were abused never go on to abuse others. I felt mildly relieved. They taught me that being a victim of child abuse was a very hard thing to get over, which explains why my flashbacks would not let up.

I was telling my story at speaking engagements across Canada and the US, and had been featured in a few documentaries. One of those documentaries, *Filling the Void*, was distributed to schools across Canada, and I felt assured that through that I was giving back. I was in another documentary, *Fight*, and that documentary benefitted kids, kids whose stories were very similar to mine, by introducing them to boxing. I was in a 26-episode APTN series, *Warriors TKO*. I'd given hundreds of talks, often traveling with my friend Brenden, and felt nothing but guilt. I was having difficulty forgiving myself for the mistakes I'd made and felt tremendous regret. I'd physically hurt people. I'd put cocaine in the hands of other addicts. The flashbacks were constant.

I reminded myself that I was doing everything I could to give back. I was doing everything I could to put positivity out into the world. If I kept doing it, the higher power would surely provide me with what I needed. Surely some positivity would come my way. When would it come my way?

Everything changed when I met my new sponsor, George. Ian and I had briefly parted ways, and I was five years sober. George instantly recognized how much pain I was in, and he had so much confidence in me that I couldn't help but have confidence in myself.

"God gave you a brain to use, so use it," he said. George made me realize I needed to grow up, and that I had it in me to get better, and to *be* better.

"Rely on yourself and your higher power," George said. "I don't want you calling me ten times a day to ask permission to go to the bathroom." It was the kick in the ass I needed, and I realized it was better to focus on solutions rather than problems.

Not long after I met George, Jaicey's mother called and asked if Jaicey could live with me. I had been sending support payments, but had been denied the opportunity to see him for the past five years.

I agreed.

He stayed with me for six months, before returning to his mom. After a few months back with his mother, Jaicey moved to Kenora to live with his aunt. Jaicey is an amazing kid, and I am happy I had those precious months with him.

CHAPTER 65

When I met Darcie, she was 8 months sober, and I was immediately attracted to her aura. She instantly became a good friend, and I joked to her that when she was one year sober, I was going to date and then marry her.

Darcie sometimes travelled with me when I'd go out of town for presentations. We'd share our stories of transformation with anyone who would listen. I trusted her implicitly, and knew that as a couple, we would have never worked.

On one of our trips up north, we went to Darcie's hometown and had dinner with her parents, Don and Vera. My first thought was, "Man, I wish I grew up in this family." As we sat down to eat, I became uncomfortable. "You're no good, Roland. This family would never want you," I thought.

On our way back to Winnipeg, Darcie could sense something was wrong. She held my hand in a friendly way, and I felt safe and protected again. I knew Darcie would never hurt me. Soon after, she let me know that my past didn't define me.

"Roland, I don't like hearing about your past," she said. "I didn't know you that way and I don't like it when you talk about it."

Bad things happened to me, and I did some bad things, but that didn't mean I was a bad person.

THE MAIN EVENT

CHAPTER 66

I received a call from the Winnipeg Chamber of Commerce in 2010. They wanted to meet with me, so I asked if they could meet me at the boxing club. When I walked into the club after work, the person at the front desk said, "There are two guys here to see you and they seem pretty fancy."

I had forgotten they were coming. I walked in and introduced myself. They asked if there was somewhere quiet we could go, so I took them to a room upstairs where I hosted recovery meetings.

They told me I had been named one of the "Top 40 Community Leaders in Winnipeg" and I was going to be featured in a book, *Winnipeg in Action*. I couldn't believe it.

"That's great, you guys, but do you mind telling me what the Winnipeg Chamber of Commerce is?"

They looked at each other and laughed. They asked me a few questions, and told me that they would be in touch as the project developed.

A few months later, I was given a copy of a book that contained profiles of the 40 people who'd been named. There's Ace Burpee! Sam Katz! My Uncle Dan! And me. There it was on paper for the world to see. I'd made a difference. Of the forty personalities profiled in the book, I was most proud to be considered as worthy as my uncle.

EPILOGUE

In 2013, I was bridged into the "Dialectical Behaviour Therapy" program through the Health Sciences Centre's psychiatric department. I'd been on the waiting list for two years, and the program was exactly what I needed.

I feel as though I am finally at a place where I am free from my past, and I am committed to enjoying the rest of my life. I'm not the person I was before, and I'm not alone.

Attitude is everything and I am by no means perfect. I lost everything once, and I won't do that again.

I have a lot of positive male role models in my life now. Growing up, I had my uncles, my hockey coaches, and Donny Lalonde, but having been abused by males, I spent many years not trusting new males in my life. The strongest people in my life have always been women.

My mother held my family together the best she could. Shannon and her mother saved my life numerous times, and have always been beacons of strength. Aunt Jeanette would always do anything she could to support me. I'm still close to Kaley and Vernelle.

My strongest supporters and closest friends are women. One of my parents' friends, Linda, is like a sister to me. I have Darcie and many other female friends, such as Candice, Lindsay, Ona Lee, Melanie, Joanne, Cindy, Rebecca, Pat, Deanna, who are like family.

While in recovery, I met and dated Stacy and Gwen, and though our relationships ended, they remain good friends and supporters.

Friends like Patty and Yvonne are powerful women who make the world a better place. Nothing brings me greater peace than riding my Harley with Patty.

I surely wouldn't be here if it wasn't for the strong women in my life. They have helped me through my darkest days, and I can't thank them enough. I know if I ever need a reality check, I just need to call Shannon or any other of my female friends, and I'll get one.

Not too long ago, Shannon sent me an e-mail. Shannon truly gets me:

> Roland, I've known you for thirty years, and I love you. Since we are best friends, I feel I can freely say this to you. You looked for loyalty and approval from your friends, you've always been that way, but you completely missed the point. It's you that is the most loyal. You surround yourself with people you can help, and you go out of your way for them when you feel down or in doubt yourself.
>
> After we divorced, you used the gang life as a surrogate family while seeking attention, affirmation and sense of belonging.
>
> As you got older, you seemed to look more and more to women for the support, and for the mothering and acceptance you needed, but never received at home. Your mother wasn't (and isn't) a bad person, but she needed to put you first, and that never seemed to happen. Each of your close female friends seems to fit a certain type. They are all nurturing. They are mothering types, the types of women you can count on, and you are most comfortable knowing there's no chance of a romantic relationship.

She's exactly right.

Many people have asked why I don't have a girlfriend. Right now, I'm committed to my youth stabilization home. It is my calling and I am devoted to my kids. In addition, I was recently named vice-president of the Red Road Lodge, a 45-bed recovery centre in Winnipeg, which helps those who are marginalized. I also spend many volunteer hours working with people who are serving time in Manitoba-based prisons and youth centres. These roles are important to me, and I don't want to force a hand if a relationship isn't in the cards. It has to be "right." The right time, the right woman, the right *me*.

I still have my setbacks, of course, but I have the strength to bounce back. I realize I spent much of my life seeking out surrogate families. Like Shannon pointed out in her e-mail, I know my parents weren't at fault, but I needed more than they could offer me.

When you choose to live in the problem, you are the problem. The axiom works both ways, and now that I live in the solution, my life is centred on positivity. I do my best every day to be a good father, a good son, and a good friend, and the rewards are fantastic.

Reality? I have the best life, and I have everything I could dream of. I'm finished my mental health commitments, and I live my life to help others. I feel strongest when I provide support to others.

Prayer has helped me to surrender and "hand it over" in times of emotional crisis. I am well aware that most of my troubles are not real and that I manufacture chaos in my head.

I've learned to forgive. I understand people make mistakes, and the greatest gift I can give myself is forgiveness. Forgiving isn't about the person who hurt you, it's about letting go of hurt. I've heard through family that my brother has built a life for himself in Alberta. We've not spoken enough for me to know what his struggles were or are, but I wish him all the best. I hope that he too has found peace.

I spent a lot of years in denial (aka "don't even notice I am lying"), and I tried to protect myself by keeping things inside. The silence hurt me more than the abuse. It festered inside me like a cancer, and I was unable to behave like a functioning human being. While I have talked a lot about my history to therapists and the like, when it comes to putting every detail in print, I have to protect my family and loved ones. Out of respect for them, I was unable to disclose everything that happened to me. That does not mean I haven't been honest here, but airing everything in these pages would only serve to sensationalize, and the minute details would serve no one well. My family and loved ones have been through enough.

I believe everyone should show their vulnerable side, as difficult as that may seem. It took me a long time, and the ability to be vulnerable only came to me in recovery. Taking that step to reach out, taking the step to trust, and finally knowing that I *can* reach out and trust people, has really changed my outlook. Had I told my parents, or a teacher, or a loved one what had happened to me, would my story have turned out the way it did? Would I have ended up nearly dead on a hotel room floor?

And therein lies the struggle. So many of us are embarrassed to ask for help. We choose to not reach out, to not share our stories, and our end result is dictated by those actions. I'm telling you now. Call. Ask. Tell someone.

Was I embarrassed to reach out for help? Did I worry about what people would think of me? If I am honest with myself, and more importantly with you, the answer to both questions is "yes." I was taught to be a "man's man," but I know now that asking for help made me stronger. Speaking the *truth* NOW makes me stronger. Facing the truth head on makes me a better man.

Being open to change, and understanding that I don't know everything, has been a saving grace in my life. I don't know everything. I'm not "the man." I'm just me.

Sure, I still worry, and I still seek approval on occasion, but my internal meltdowns are few and far between. I can go months without doubting myself, or questioning others' motives. But when the storm comes, I have mechanisms in place that allow me to cope. I have friends. I have family. I have supports.

Not that long ago, I e-mailed Dr Simm to ask if I was still his patient. I think it will be good for me to resume our visits. I want to be preventative, so that if I ever feel overwhelmed, I'll remember that what I thought was the end turned out to be the beginning of my life.

The real *beginning of my life.*

And what a life it is. I was recently nominated for a Manitoba Human Rights Award, and my youth foster stabilization home is considered one of the best placements in the province. I've coached Team Manitoba's boxing athletes, and I was named one of Manitoba's Most Fascinating People in 2013. I have given over 700 motivational speeches, and helped others with my story. There's a new documentary about my life, and a feature film in the works. Through writing this book, I've met a few more people who I know are in my corner, and I'm in theirs. I have family and friends who love me.) The darkest days of my life are well in the past.

I've climbed back into the ring of life, and I'm not just a contender. I'm winning.

Bring it on. I have a lot of knockout punches to throw.

To see a man beaten not by a better opponent
but by himself is a tragedy.
—Cus D'Amato, boxing manager and trainer

APPENDIX

DR SIMM ON ADDICTION AND PTSD

In my over 25 years in the field of psychiatry, as both a psychiatric nurse and an addiction psychiatrist, I have seen hundreds, if not thousands, of men and women struggling with addictions and PTSD. Some surveys estimate as many as half the people seeking treatment for substance abuse also have PTSD (*Brady Current Dir Psych Sci*, 2004). They present a unique challenge for care providers. Which disorder should be treated first? Should the patient "relive" the trauma in therapy? What works for patients? Maybe they shouldn't stop using substances or engaging in their addictive behaviour if that is the only thing that helps them.

Why do people keep on using substances when everyone, including the patient, can see the addiction is destroying their life? Many theories have been postulated, but in my opinion, the answer is simple. Drugs and alcohol work! They erase memories, calm the internal storms, allow one to sleep, and bolster self-confidence and self-esteem. Many find "normal interactions" impossible without them. Not only do they work, but the results are quick and easy. Improvement is seen almost immediately, and all that has to be done is to get the chemical of choice into the body.

The cure is short-lived. Soon the effects wear off. The PTSD is still there and often worse. The temporary mood-elevating effects experienced have a payback. The neurotransmitters, such as dopamine, that are in part responsible for experiencing pleasure have been depleted, and restlessness, irritability and discontent return. The social consequences of substance use are numerous: lost friends, lost jobs, lost physical health, lost finances, etc. The belief that one can overcome their emotional pain through perseverance and hard work is gone. Life is overwhelming, what can possibly help? The answer is obvious: a return to the substances. And the cycle continues.

No easy answers exist. In fact, for many, despite many attempts at treatment, their addictions and PTSD symptoms continue. In my experience working with this population, some common factors arise in those successful in overcoming their addictions.

All PTSD is not the same. There are those with the "classical" onset and symptoms of PTSD. The person who has had a single traumatic episode such as an assault, motor vehicle accident or house fire and tries to erase the memories of the incident through use of drugs and alcohol usually has a better prognosis than those who have suffered from ongoing repeated stressors (such as soldiers in a combat zone). Those with a single episode of trauma generally have their personality intact. The chronic stress seems to eat away at the positive aspects of one's personality that are needed to overcome the use of substances. Those with chronic stressors often lose the hope, faith and courage that is needed for therapy and recovery.

A special population of PTSD and substance abusers are those who have suffered ongoing child abuse. These may be the most difficult to help. The basic elements of trust in others, and the belief in one's own abilities, are established early in life. The abused child learns to see the world as cruel and evil, and often believe others exist only to cause them pain. Establishing a positive working relationship in treatment is close to impossible. Substance use often starts very early in life for this population. Important developmental milestones are never reached as time is spent using drugs and alcohol.

There is some evidence the natural maturing of the brain that continues to occur throughout the teenage years is stunted with early use of substances. Without this natural maturing, adult decision making is impossible.

Successful treatment for those with addictions and childhood trauma is a journey that will take years. Accepting this, and realizing that it will often be two steps forward, one step back, is of critical importance. Expecting the latest antidepressant and a few words of comfort from a counsellor will have long-lasting effects will lead to disappointment and failure.

I have found that patients who become actively involved in 12 step groups and establish stable sobriety before undergoing intensive therapy addressing their childhood experiences have the best prognosis. While one is beginning to establish sobriety, therapy is best limited to general principles such as accepting you were not responsible for the trauma and abuse of your childhood; that you are a valuable, worthwhile person; and learning "grounding techniques" when feeling overwhelmed with emotions and memories of the abuse.

Twelve-step groups provide supports that are not easily found elsewhere. Availability is unmatched by any organization I am aware of. Meetings can be found seven days a week, several times a day in all major cities. Even smaller communities have readily available meetings. The atmosphere is friendly and supportive. As with any other organization, if you look for negative influences you can find them, but the positive far outweighs the negative.

Twelve-step groups provide the initial structure to help attain sobriety. Fellow members have been through those difficult early days and instinctively know when gentle support is needed and when a firm "reality check" is called for. Members have practical simple suggestions to help stay clean and sober when your mind and body are crying out for one more high.

As a member progresses through AA, or any other 12 step program, not only do they establish their sobriety, but a maturing of the personality begins to occur. Issues of spirituality are reflected upon. For many this is a sticking point, many proclaim they are atheists/agnostics and don't want "religion crammed down my throat." However, the most important part about spirituality is not that the member believe in "God as we understood him," but to realize that they themselves are not Gods and the world does not revolve around them.

The 12 steps encourage one to accept they are human and like all humans have flaws, but this does not make them worthless or hopeless. The steps encourage working with others, taking responsibility for behaviour, and developing a sense of self-worth accompanied by a dose of humility. Members learn to accept constructive feedback and are able to put temporary setbacks in perspective.

With abstinence firmly established and the personality strengthened, the member is ready to fully benefit from more intensive self-exploration.

There are many misconceptions about AA and its interaction with psychiatry. One common misconception is that AA frowns upon the use of any psychotropic medications. While individual members have their opinions regarding medications, AA accepts that this is a matter between the member and their doctor. In my own experience, many who believe they require medication for anxiety and depression when they first seek treatment find they do quite well without it after a month of sobriety. In fact, early prescription of medication seems to lead some to believe there is an easy path to happiness and sobriety, and to avoid the hard work that is needed to achieve both. While there are always exceptions (especially when people suffer from psychosis or mania), as a general rule, psychiatric medications other than those needed for withdrawal should be avoided for the first month of sobriety.

One other common misconception is that psychiatrists do not believe in the principles of AA and will dissuade the member from attending. Again, this is far from the truth. Most psychiatrists realize the valuable support that AA provides and will encourage their patient to attend. Bill Wilson, co-founder of AA, wrote that regular attendance helps the member develop the self-awareness and inner strength to fully benefit from psychotherapy. In my own experience, I have found that members with at least a year of sobriety and regular attendance are able to handle reliving childhood memories, or receiving constructive feedback and criticism without lashing out in anger, stopping therapy, or relapsing.

Those who have suffered from childhood abuse and turned to addictions to ease their inner pain have pathways open that can lead to recovery. The road may be long, the journey a challenge, but the rewards are immeasurable. Twelve-step groups and psychiatry can work together with those for suffer from these all too common disorders.